ASK IWATA

Iwata-San

WORDS OF WISDOM
FROM **SATORU IWATA**
NINTENDO'S LEGENDARY CEO

ASK
IWATA

Edited by **HOBONICHI**
Translated by **SAM BETT**

ASK IWATA

IWATASAN: IWATA SATORU WA KONNAKOTO WO HANASHITEITA.
by Satoru Iwata and Hobonichi Co., Ltd.
ILLUSTRATED BY **100%ORANGE**

COPYRIGHT © **Satoru Iwata** © **Hobonichi, 2019**
ILLUSTRATIONS COPYRIGHT © **100%ORANGE, 2019**
All rights reserved.

ORIGINAL JAPANESE EDITION PUBLISHED BY **Hobonichi Co., Ltd.**

This English edition is published by arrangement
with Hobonichi Co., Ltd. Tokyo in care of Tuttle-Mori
Agency, Inc., Tokyo

THIS EDITION PUBLISHED BY **VIZ Media, LLC**
P.O. Box 77010 | San Francisco, CA 94107

ENGLISH TRANSLATION **Sam Bett**
DESIGN & LAYOUT **Francesca Truman**

Library of Congress Cataloging-in-Publication
Data available.

ISBN: 978-1-9747-2154-2

10 9 8 7 6 5 4 3 2 1

Printed in the United States of America.

viz.com

" On my business card, I am a corporate president. In my mind, I am a game developer. But in my heart, I am a gamer. **"**

SATORU IWATA

TABLE OF CONTENTS

PREFACE
xi

CHAPTER ONE
IWATA, FUTURE PRESIDENT

CHAPTER TWO
THE LEADERSHIP OF IWATA

CHAPTER THREE
IWATA, THE INDIVIDUAL

CHAPTER FOUR
THE PEOPLE IWATA BELIEVES IN

CHAPTER FIVE
THE GAMES IWATA STRIVES TO MAKE

CHAPTER SIX
REMEMBERING IWATA

CHAPTER SEVEN
IWATA, THE PERSON

PREFACE

This book presents assorted reflections from Satoru Iwata that were originally published on the website *Hobo Nikkan Itoi Shinbun*. A portion of the text also draws from the "Iwata Asks" column serialized on the Nintendo website. Iwata rarely talked about himself when interacting with the media. When he believed that the company or project would benefit the most if he were the one to speak, he stepped up to the mic, but any discussion of his personal experience was usually coincidental.

That said, as so many of us are well aware, Iwata was an extremely honest and resolute individual. If you gather together his various remarks—made on a variety of occasions in his capacity as chief executive or as the head of development—his personal insights naturally come to the fore, in a synergy of insight and experience.

This book aims to bring those insights together, gathering into a single volume Iwata's words of wisdom from a multitude of articles.

Iwata passed away on July 11, 2015. He was a kind man, who in his years at HAL Laboratory distinguished himself as a programmer by creating a score of iconic games, and as the president of Nintendo gave the world such consoles as the Nintendo DS and Wii in an earnest effort to, as he put it, "expand the gaming population." News of his death weighed heavily on the hearts of people the world over.

From its inception in 1998, *Hobo Nikkan Itoi Shinbun* was lucky enough to have Iwata as a collaborator. He and Shigesato Itoi, our editor in chief, happened to be extremely close, and on occasion Iwata paid a visit to our office to chat with Itoi for as much time as his schedule allowed. He was more than happy to take part in a number of articles we produced, and frequently approached us with content he produced himself.

His sudden passing left us distraught, like so many other game lovers across the world. It felt like a piece of our hearts had been taken away.

Now, several years have passed, and though we have recovered slightly from the pain, there's something missing in our lives without Iwata around. This feeling prompted us to give Iwata new life through this book. It was the least that we could do, with all the words of wisdom that he gave us.

As a note on what follows, most of the source material for this book can still be found in a perusal of our website. If you read carefully through the articles and interviews, you're bound to find something familiar. Yet it's inevitable for web content to be buried under new material, and pretty soon nobody reads it anymore.

We're confident that people out there would welcome the chance to revisit what Iwata had to say, and we think the number of people seeking to learn more about Iwata, and understand him on a personal level, will only continue to increase.

In his lifetime, Iwata expressed a lack of interest in publishing a book, though he did receive offers. And while we may anticipate a strong demand, both now and in the future, for a book compiling Iwata's observations, we recognize that in a sense we're taking liberties.

All the same, we believe that Iwata would give his blessing to the book we have created. He liked to offer his opinion when in trusted company, and grinned whenever he read through the latest article. (Although he may well have asked us, "Are you sure making a book like this is worth everyone's time?")

A number of individuals were indispensable to the creation of this book. To the employees of Nintendo, to Shigeru Miyamoto, to Iwata's longtime secretary, Reiko Wakimoto, and to Iwata's wife and his entire family, thank you for permitting us to include the material in this book.

Iwata, our dear friend. Sometimes we find ourselves wanting to call out your name. It seems like any day you might crack open the office door, wearing that grin of yours. It's devastating to consider that we'll never be able to catch up with you again.

Every page of this book is suffused with Iwata's thinking and philosophy. His words continue to steel our resolve, showing us how to live an honest life.

May the words of Satoru Iwata continue to reach new audiences for years to come.

_____

HOBO NIKKAN ITOI SHINBUN
JULY 2019

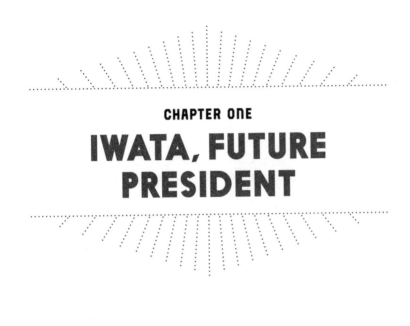

CHAPTER ONE

IWATA, FUTURE PRESIDENT

High school years: Discovering the programmable calculator

In high school, before anyone had even heard of a PC, I discovered something known as a "programmable calculator." I used to make games during class and play them with a friend who sat beside me. Looking back, this was my first encounter with games or programming.

That calculator was made by Hewlett-Packard. Astronauts brought these devices on the Apollo-Soyuz Test Project, and are said to have used them to calculate the angle of their antennas. At the time, they were really expensive, but once I'd saved up half the money working part-time washing dishes, my father agreed to chip in the rest.

I went crazy for this calculator. I had no hobbyist magazine to turn to and nobody to teach me, so I had to figure things out on my own. Through trial and error, I came to realize, "Hey, I can do this, and I can do that, too."

In retrospect, this was a pretty unique calculator. First off, it had no equals key. If you were adding one plus two, you pressed 1, then hit enter. After that, you would press 2, and finally the plus key. This way of inputting the numbers reminded me of Japanese word order, where it would sound something like this: "If one and two are added, and that and four are multiplied, and twelve is subtracted, what do you get?" The only thing missing was the equals sign, and I don't think most people actually missed it. I was hooked on figuring out how to use this thing like a pro.

Playing around, I managed to create a game, and sent it to the Hewlett-Packard distributor in Japan. They were absolutely baffled. They must have been like, "Whoa, what's this high school whiz kid doing up in Sapporo?" Speaking from experience, this would be like if some high schooler sent Nintendo a totally finished game that we could put on shelves tomorrow. They must have been amazed. It's funny—at the time, I had no idea whatsoever just how valuable this thing that I had made actually was.

About two years after I got hooked on that calculator, Apple released its first desktop computer out into the world.

But as soon as I was able to test out one of these new computers, my fantasies evaporated. I realized the computer was not some dream machine, capable of anything. To put it differently, while I was still in high school, I got a pretty good grasp of what computers were good for, and what they were not so good for.

I'm really lucky that I had a friend seated beside me who enjoyed the games that I was making on my calculator.

That friend was a pretty interesting guy ... in a sense, I suppose he was the first person to appreciate my work. My very first customer. User number one.

As human beings, unless we have someone to compliment our work and enjoy what we've created, we're not apt to go out on a limb. Which is why meeting this friend in high school had such a positive effect on the course of my life.

College years: Making friends at the computer store

In my first year of college, which would have been 1978, the first computer department at perhaps any store in Japan opened at the Seibu Department Store in Ikebukuro. I made the trek there every weekend.

In those days, people used to spend the whole day hanging out at the computer store, sitting at the computers and writing programs. Most people couldn't afford to buy a computer themselves.

To buy mine, I had spent all of my savings and the money I was given when I entered college, and I had even taken on a loan. My first computer was a PET, made by a company called Commodore.

They sold them at the Seibu Department Store in Ikebukuro, which was where I started going with the programs I was making. Because my high school friend who played my calculator games had gone off to a different university, I lacked companionship.

I think it was as simple as wanting to show somebody my creations. If I visited the Seibu computer store, there was always someone there who shared my interests and was a receptive audience.

I made some very important connections at that store, foremost of these with a distinguished programmer who turned out to be the strongest motivator for my future work.

One day, he was using a computer at the store to write a program, but something wasn't working right. He looked frustrated. Glancing over his shoulder, I realized, "There's your problem."

I told him, "Hey, if you fix this, I think it'll work."

"Right," he said, "of course."

After that, we were fast friends. He was in his second year of college, and I was in my first.

The gang of us that used the computers at the store spontaneously formed a user group. We also befriended the manager, who wound up starting his own company when I was in my third year.

That company was HAL Laboratory.

"I'm starting a company," he said. "Want a part-time job?" That was the beginning of my career as a programmer. I found the work so fascinating that I stuck around.

And so, by chance, HAL Laboratory secured a reputation as a home for part-time employees who could hold their own against the pros.

After four years at university, I graduated on time. I wasn't exactly the best student, though. It was pretty hard to focus on my studies when I was having so much fun working at HAL!

My college coursework helped me understand the basics of computing. I'm glad I went, but most of the work that I did later on was a continuation of the things I'd taught myself.

The dawn of HAL Laboratory and the release of the Famicom

Since I was already working part-time at HAL, I was able to move up into a full-time position as soon as I graduated university. This was an ideal opportunity, since I enjoyed what I was doing so much that it didn't feel like work.

With its small size, HAL Laboratory gave me the chance at a young age to make all kinds of important decisions. Crucially, there was nobody above me working on development, which made me the point person by default. As a result, I had to handle all development matters myself. There was nobody to turn to for advice.

This led to yet another chance encounter. A year after I became a proper employee, Nintendo released the Famicom (short for "Family Computer," later updated and sold outside of Japan as the Nintendo Entertainment System).

I had been developing computer games since my days as a part-timer, but the Famicom gave us a totally new platform, changing forever the way that games would be made.

At the time, a PC in Japan would cost you a small fortune, but the Famicom was only 15,000 yen, making it the obvious choice as a platform for playing games. I had a feeling that this system was going to change the world. I knew right away: "I need to find a way to get involved."

As it so happened, there was somebody connected with Nintendo at one of the companies investing in HAL Laboratory, and that person was kind enough to introduce me. With my heart set on doing something for the Famicom, pretty soon I found myself visiting Nintendo headquarters in Kyoto.

I was in my early twenties. Dressed in a suit I clearly wasn't used to wearing, I showed up out of nowhere, just some newbie, and said, "Please, let us work on something." I felt a little bold asking for work like that, but in retrospect, I realize they were making themselves vulnerable too!

They enlisted us to program software for their games. This was the start of my relationship with Nintendo. Some of the early Famicom releases such as *Pinball* and *Golf* were made by me and the folks at HAL.

Making games for the Famicom was loads of fun, especially when they started selling like crazy all around the world. Since those games were designed on commission, we didn't benefit financially from the sales, but we were overjoyed that our games had become household names. These creations that, once upon a time, had only been known to the friend seated next to me had reached people all over the world. What could be cooler than that?

By linking up with the Famicom soon after its release, we were fortunate enough to play a substantial role in the widespread growth of that particular game console. In ten years, HAL Laboratory went from a mere five employees to as many as ninety.

I was basically responsible for development, and soon the title of manager was on my business card. Eventually, they started calling me director of development.

Looking back, the games that we developed in those days all involved big software ideas where the client wasn't quite sure how to pull it off. Once we had made something of a name for ourselves, we were lauded for our technical abilities, which led to a steady stream of work.

Becoming president with 1.5 billion yen of debt

When I was thirty-two years old, HAL Laboratory ran into financial difficulties. Then, when I was thirty-three, I was promoted to president, but since the company was on shaky ground this was no time for celebration.

Simply put, I became president because we had no other option. Whether I was for it or against it didn't matter. When I'm convinced that I'm the best person for the job, I step up to the plate.

Broadly speaking, the company was going under, and on my first day as president, we had 1.5 billion yen of debt.

In the end, we paid it off over six years, shelling out 250,000,000 yen annually. Of course, we had to cover all our operating costs, so in order to compensate our employees and keep the lights on, we took on a separate line of debt.

Eventually we paid everything off, but the process was a burden on a lot of people, so I can't exactly say I'm proud of the experience.

Without a doubt, though, this experience was valuable. Carrying such an immense amount of debt throws everything into sharp relief, especially how people treat each other.

This reminds me of when I was going around to different banks, soon after becoming president. I was basically still a kid—in my early thirties—stopping by to say, "I recently became the president, and I'm committed to paying off this debt." Some of the banks said, "We know you can do it." But others said, "If you can't pay this off, it's your neck on the line," really cranking up the pressure.

What's incredibly interesting is that the bankers who put the most pressure on me were the most likely to be gone when I went back. Things turned out to be just as grave for them.

But things weren't only difficult with people from outside the company.

After we found ourselves in dire straits, and I took over as president and tried to make things right, the staff gave me the benefit of the doubt, since I had won their trust as the most well-rounded member of the development team. On the flip side, everyone had basically lost faith in the company. Let's put it this way: if your company is on the brink of bankruptcy, all you can see as one of its employees is a heap of problems. After all, it's only natural to look at things and say, "Is this what happens when we take orders from corporate?"

This is why I spent my first month as president interviewing everybody at the company. The discoveries were endless.

My plan was to be a sounding board and to get a sense of what was happening, but when I sat down with each person individually, I was blown away by how much I was learning. The idea was to figure out everybody's strengths and weaknesses. Without this kind of knowledge, I knew I couldn't make decisions on behalf of the whole company.

When we talk about a piece of programming, we gauge its merits based on how short or economical or fast it is. As the ultimate decision maker, I wanted to establish criteria for evaluating things, so I started off by interviewing every person at the company. The variety of perspectives this uncovered was astounding.

I came to find out that management is not so simple after all, and chasing short-term earnings is not always the appropriate strategy. I had to wonder, "How can we turn things around?" Once the company fell into difficult economic circumstances, this became a driving question.

It was during these interviews that I realized that decision-making means gathering and analyzing information and managing priorities, and that as you discover your priorities, you should see where they take you as you work through your decisions.

If you take this approach to decision-making, things will gradually come together. This strikes me as a principle with general applicability. I know it's gone a long way in establishing trust in me as president.

There are so many things that I can see today that I couldn't see back then, which helps me to appreciate the difficulty of the challenges I faced when I was thirty-three.

Interviewing every employee twice a year

When a company is in trouble, everything is an emergency. The thought on everybody's mind is, "If we don't finish this thing in a week, we're toast!" However, once you declare bankruptcy, you're able to slow down and take your time, allowing you to do the things you couldn't do before.

For me, the thing I couldn't do before was meeting every single employee and talking with each person one-on-one.

Once I did that, I made so many discoveries and realized that this should have been a top priority all along. Even once we had the company back on its feet and business re-turned to normal, I never gave up these dialogues with every member of the staff.

In my time as president of HAL Laboratory, I spoke with each employee twice a year. This sometimes meant as many as eighty or ninety individuals. The time varied per person, with some meetings as short as twenty minutes and some people talking for almost three hours. I kept this up for six or seven years.

The first time I sat down with everyone, there were a huge number of things I had never heard until doing these interviews. Even the folks I thought had been communicating fairly well shared things I'd been unaware of until we sat down individually. As strange as it sounds, I realized that until someone has nothing left to lose, they won't ever open up to you like this.

Normally, I'm of the view that if a person hasn't given you an opportunity, it's up to you to make one and approach them. I saw us as the sort of group that didn't need to schedule check-ins, and I thought if something needed to be said, people would speak up as necessity demanded. But as it turns out, not every person at a company is like this.

Ask me what sort of company I would want to work for, and I would say "A place where my boss understands me" or "A place where my boss cares about my quality of life."

I also believe that everyone is different and always changing. Sure, lots of people never change. But I would never want to work under a leader who failed to understand that people can evolve.

I would want a boss who pays attention and acknowledges my growth. Which is why I always tried to understand the other members of the company. This was the motive behind the interviews. It wasn't easy, but I realized there was much I could gain from them.

As I sat down with each of the employees, I found that everybody touched on different themes. The only constant from one interview to the next was my opening question: "Are you happy doing what you're doing?"

I had no plans of harping on about a corporate vision or the like, but as I carried out the interviews, I began to realize something: since the whole point of a company was for people to work together toward a common goal by combining their strengths, I should clarify our goal.

To that end, I offered this: "The mission of HAL Laboratory is to bring happiness to our customers—who play the games—and to our employees—who make them—through our products."

Once this was established, the question "Are you happy doing what you're doing?" had some context. But when I asked people this question, they had all kinds of answers, as you can imagine.

Without mutual sympathy and understanding, I see no point in this kind of dialogue. Which is why if someone had complaints, I made sure to hear them out. However, as I listened to what they had to say, I would always speak up when I had something to say myself.

The more frustrated someone is, the more important it becomes to listen to them. Unless you make a point of this, anything you try to say goes in one ear and out the other. If you interrupt them midsentence and say, "It's more like this," it's only natural for them to think, "This person has absolutely no clue what I'm saying."

If you let people tell you what they want to say, and wait for them to finish, they'll give you a chance to weigh in afterward.

I believe that whether people decide to accept what they are told or not is entirely based on whether they think "You're only saying this to benefit yourself" or "You're saying this because, deep down, you believe it."

This is why I think that management depends on an ability to minimize your personal agenda.

Self-serving behavior has never been a part of how I work. Sure, I've done my share of negotiating, and I'm not pretending that some give-and-take isn't essential to making a deal, but when it comes to the people you see every day at work, it's best to keep things transparent.

Everybody wants to have a say. Still, whenever a company makes a bunch of decisions, most of the people working there won't understand where those decisions came from. Simply put, there's a lack of information.

"Did you hear what the president said? What's that all about?" This sort of question pops up all the time.

Listening to people speak their minds one-on-one, I came to realize "The reason behind that particular decision isn't getting through" or "That thing I said was misconstrued and became a real source of frustration." Where possible, I took these opportunities to provide additional context for why I'd said what I had said, or what events had led to a particular decision.

Effectively, this was the same as asking them, "Given these circumstances, what would have been your thoughts?" When somebody says, "I would have done the same thing," of course it's reassuring. Discovering a shared set of values makes both parties feel a lot more comfortable.

When there has been a misunderstanding, or someone doesn't feel the same way about things, I think it's generally because of a handful of predictable factors. When these factors combine to form patterns, people grow hostile toward one another and get angry, cry, or become depressed. This usually means a number of factors have tangled together, but if you work through them one by one, rooting out the problem, everybody comes away feeling relieved.

The length of the interview depends on when we reach this point. When the person feels relieved, we wrap things up. This means we talk until we get there. I make a point of that.

I think that keeping up these interviews is an enormous part of what made everybody put their trust in me. It's not the sort of thing you can continue doing just for show, and everyone could see just how much energy it took.

Running away would mean a lifetime of regret

I always made an effort, whether it was with our customers or with the other companies that gave us work, to deliver a product that exceeded their expectations.

When HAL Laboratory was in financial trouble, people from the companies that had worked with us repeatedly reached out and said, "We'll do anything we can to help, just say the word," and in fact, not a single company tried to break their contract with us.

In retrospect, this difficult period was an incredible learning experience for me. You'd think that, under the circumstances, people might say things like, "Don't go to them, they can't be trusted," but that's not how things turned out for us.

When our future was uncertain, and we were saddled with over a billion yen in liabilities, the first option was to run away. But I dismissed this as a possibility.

Running away would mean a lifetime of regret. The reasoning behind my decision ultimately came down to this.

Considering our estimated value, carrying over a billion yen in debt was out of the question. Was my decision not to run about ethics or aesthetics? It's hard to say, but perhaps a little of both. The biggest sticking point for me was this: How could I run away after everything my friends and I had been through?

I'm thankful for my wife, who never questioned my decision to become president of a company carrying an exorbitant amount of debt.

Things did not look good at all. As my life partner, she was taking on an enormous risk as well. It would have been perfectly reasonable for her to say, "Do you really have to do this?" But she never said a word. For that, I'm truly thankful.

As president, I continued to look after development. When I asked myself "What are this company's strengths?" the answer was clear: leveraging development was our sole hope of turning things around. This took me all of ten seconds to realize.

At that point, I had resolved to be wherever the action was. The company had several different teams, with staggered busy periods, so I made sure I was around to support the busiest team at any given time.

I did this because at the time, as head developer for the company, I had the strongest ability to discover, analyze, and resolve the various problems we were facing.

Aiding the most desperate areas of the company made sense in terms of productivity, while at the same time, if I wanted to demonstrate that I was taking care of business, nothing beat actually showing up and solving problems on the spot. There was no better way of getting folks to say, "With him behind the wheel, we're in good hands."

From my vantage point at the top of development, I could see the entire company. Especially back then, our batting average with video games was high, so as long as we made something good, we knew that it would sell. My hands-on connection with development was a bonus for all kinds of reasons. This was the golden age of the Super Famicom.

The company got a lucky break and managed to spring back to life with *Kirby's Dream Land*.

It was originally slated to come out on Game Boy under the title *Twinkle Popo*, but Shigeru Miyamoto told us,

"This game deserves more attention." So we put off its release and made a few tweaks and fixes, and eventually it was reborn as *Kirby's Dream Land*, the first game in what became the *Kirby* series from Nintendo.

Meanwhile, the ads for *Twinkle Popo* had gone up on schedule, and the orders had been coming in—around twenty-six thousand, in fact. When we canceled the release, it caused a scandal at the company, as you can imagine. From the perspective of the folks in sales, it was a mortal blow to our reputation.

In reality, though, we wound up selling over five million units of *Kirby's Dream Land* for the Game Boy. A quick calculation shows this to be over two hundred times the number of initial orders.

Clearly, if we hadn't canceled the release, the *Kirby* series as we know it never would have come to be. Across the entire series, these games have achieved cumulative sales of over twenty million units worldwide, and if you include the *Super Smash Bros.* series, where Kirby features as a character, the sales have easily exceeded thirty million units [as of 2005], making our decision to delay a truly pivotal event.

IWATA'S WORDS OF WISDOM
PART ONE

- When I was little, I was sick a lot and had asthma, and after I switched schools, I was bullied for a while. Through these experiences, I saw the world through the eyes of the weak. My first job happened to be at a small company that was weaker, by comparison, than larger companies. But seeing the world through the eyes of the weak was an incredibly valuable experience for me. Even after becoming president of Nintendo, which was far from a weak position, I could never lose sight of my earlier experiences, nor do I look back on those hard times and feel any resentment whatsoever.

- When I was president of HAL Laboratory, I wholeheartedly believed that if another person would make a better president, I would want that individual to take my place.

- Since my background is in development, I am better able to understand the mind of someone working in development than the average executive.

- If a president says they'll revolutionize the industry, but for the next five years the company won't be able to turn a profit, they'll find themselves without a job. And so, every year, they need to generate a steady stream of profits, but they also need to innovate. It's like flying along in an airplane and working on repairs midflight.

- When I look back on things, it's hard for me to tell whether I chose a unique path because I'm different, or chose a unique path by chance, and became who I am. What I will say is I've been extremely lucky to find my way into environments that have suited me so well—beyond that, I'm not so sure.

- I used to be on the programming side of making games. Now I develop new hardware and platforms. My work has changed tremendously, in volume and substance, but deep down, my mentality and stance are basically the same. I may no longer be a programmer, sitting down with everyone and writing programs, but I'll always count myself as one of the creators.

- What are our strengths? What are our weaknesses? Management means figuring this out and leading the company in a direction that helps everyone's strengths flourish and keeps their weaknesses in check.

CHAPTER TWO

THE LEADERSHIP OF IWATA

What do we do well?

The number of things we should be doing is always greater than what we can actually do. If you try doing everything on your list, you'll only wear yourself out.

Which is why an awareness of a group's collective strengths will help you clarify priorities. I think setting things in place is what management is all about.

Well then, what exactly do we mean by collective strengths? Here's how I see it.

At work, it may feel like everyone is making a consistent effort, but sometimes the client will surprise you and be more excited or less excited than anticipated—even if the amount of time and energy you've all invested was the same as usual. You can give two jobs 100 percent, but one client will see it as 100 percent, and another will see it as 500 percent.

To paraphrase, sometimes the work will be extremely difficult, while other times it's not so bad. Work always involves some level of difficulty. Otherwise, we wouldn't call it work. When the going gets tough, if we're not praised accordingly for our efforts, it makes things even harder. When things enter a downward spiral, people's spirits flag all around, and speaking with staff becomes essential. Conversely, when the company is praised out of proportion for its efforts, it starts to feel like everyone can breathe more easily and relax.

And so, when the whole group can earn praise without working insanely hard, things get better and better on their own, creating a virtuous cycle where the work only gets stronger. This means the group has tapped into their strengths. When this doesn't happen, my usual assessment is the work isn't for them.

Oftentimes, people compare their good work against someone else's not-so-good work and complain, "This is unfair—I'm not getting the credit I deserve." Even I catch myself doing this from time to time.

This is just a personal opinion, but isn't the ultimate goal of all living things to propagate the species? If we want to propagate the species, each of us needs to make a point of why we do this one thing better than anybody else. In other words, an ability to assert "I am better at this skill than other people" is in the DNA all around us. Those without that kind of strength have gradually disappeared from the gene pool.

Hence, all living things have an innate ability to assert their unique abilities. At an organization like a company, everyone is prone to view their own strengths favorably against the weaknesses of others.

However, unless people have a shared understanding of the company as a place where praise and criticism have a specific purpose, before long things will seem unfair.

When things aren't working out, it's best to call it quits. No task is right for everyone. Still, to some degree we need to hang in there. If we were to collectively decide to stop doing all the things that we dislike, the company would collapse.

And so, in essence, a company can aspire to be a group focused on the things that it does best, but in order for people to work together it's imperative to figure out the bare minimum of operating tasks that need to be completed, regardless of how taxing or unpleasant they may be. In that respect, I think it's up to the management to ensure that this bare minimum is as small as possible.

After all, the whole point of a company is for regular people, each with their distinctive characteristics, to join forces and accomplish giant tasks they could not undertake alone.

Locating the bottlenecks

Computers have been able to develop swiftly because of the sheer volume of trial and error they are able to process.

When tweaking the mold for a piece of hardware, it takes an extraordinary amount of time to try out several different types. But when it comes to software, you can test something like "How high does Mario have to jump for people to enjoy the game?" repeatedly over the course of a day.

Nothing ever starts out perfect. It's all about repeated trial and error. You try out different things and realize, "Oh, that's better, let's do that," gradually improving the overall design.

And when large numbers of people have a hand in the same project, some tasks are divided easily and some are not. Even complex atmospheric simulations can be achieved at greater speed when they're divided into various parts and concurrently programmed for separate processors. But sometimes one task will influence the operation of another, and that task will wind up influencing the first, making it impossible to work concurrently.

Any job will wind up having bottlenecks, these areas with little wiggle room that limit the overall scope of the project. Meanwhile, if you want to make any big picture changes, the first thing you need to do is find the bottlenecks and fix them. You can fix as many of the looser areas as you like, but the general design will barely change.

This is something I have come to understand on a deep level. It's one of the reasons I was so comfortable working with computers.

If the goal is to make the program faster, there will always be a bottleneck to blame for slowing down the operation.

In programs, it's possible for a given process to be executed so repeatedly that it would be fair to say that 1 percent of the entire program eats up 70 to 80 percent of the total processing time. As a result, until you've cleared up all the bottlenecks, it's meaningless to try to speed up any other parts.

The trouble is that people feel better when they have their hands full, so until they find the bottlenecks, they tend to sweat over whatever issues they encounter. Before taking any action, you should identify the most problematic areas and figure out what you, and only you, can do to fix them.

Even taking this approach, your starting point is never more than a hypothesis, which you may soon discover to be wrong. Ideally, you'd start off saying, "Okay, this has to be a bottleneck, so if I change this then the whole thing will improve," and then proceed accordingly, but more often than not, this isn't possible.

In my opinion, there is a huge amount of overlap between the world of solo programmers and the world of more collaborative work, and identifying these overlaps can teach us all kinds of things. I've found this perspective to be extremely useful in figuring things out, analyzing difficult problems, and uncovering solutions.

The taste of success brings resistance to change

Some organizations out there have enjoyed success by maintaining the same mission and philosophy for several years and succeeding over and over again.

Successful organizations have a tendency to be terrified of change, but lately I've been extremely conscious of how quickly things can transform. These days, we're seeing huge changes to all kinds of environments, incredible changes to the way that people think and how information is distributed.

As we realign our processes to be more sensitive to changes in the world around us, this has led not only myself but people all across the company to ask, "Is what we think of as the best way of doing things actually correct?"

The needs of customers change, as does the climate of the market, the ways we share information, the content people want to see, the people buying the games, and the kinds of stores that sell them. Everything is always changing, is always in a state of flux.

And yet, I don't believe successful organizations need to fix what isn't broken. Their employees have been working all along with the best intentions and have achieved success in the process, so rejecting the status quo will not encourage sympathy or understanding.

Every kind of change involves rejection of the status quo, but such rejection promises to make many people unhappy. After all, it took them a tremendous amount of hope and frank enthusiasm to get to where they are. While I believe we should hold those with bad intentions accountable, I also believe we should avoid outright rejection of the results of good intentions.

There are things about the current climate of Nintendo that I think should change, but I don't think we should start off by negating the current situation.

If things get to the point where the company will fall apart if left to its own devices, and a reason to change is staring everybody in the face ... no one is going to protest a rejection of the status quo. But situations this extreme are rare.

Obviously, Nintendo is not in a situation where I would want to turn things upside down.

I have immense respect for the last president of Nintendo, Hiroshi Yamauchi. He took the company to incredible heights I couldn't possibly have reached, setting a standard that I'm always struggling to meet.

At the same time, as his successor I was left with a large number of pressing tasks, and taking care of these things while encouraging sympathy and understanding meant I needed to choose a very prudent tack.

While I'm interested in making a large number of changes, I don't make changes from a spirit of rejection. Rather, my feeling is this: "If I was at Nintendo in the old days, I would have taken the same course of action that led to what we're doing now." But times have changed. The world has changed around us. If we don't change too, what's going to happen? Should we take a path of gradual obscurity? Or should we take the path of the future, enabling more people than ever to enjoy the things we make?

Shocking people, in a good way

When we test out the things we make, people have no interest whatsoever, not even a little bit. This is how it always is, in the beginning.

From there, unless we can win people over, improving products so much that people pick them up and smile, we've failed. It's not enough to make a big splash and move units. Unless you can come up with something new six months or one year down the line and make customers say, "Wow, before I knew it I was playing all the time," you're done. If you fail in that respect, you haven't actually accomplished your objective.

After a product goes on sale, you may have a second or third string to your bow, but you have to wonder: Will you really hit the target? Will you reach the hearts of your customers? Will they continue playing? I always try to tell myself it's going to be okay.

Meanwhile, if you rely on what we might call a short-sighted cleverness, making decisions solely by comparing options and deciding "This one's better," you're bound to wind up on the road more often traveled. A major reason why this hasn't happened to Nintendo is that we've maintained clear objectives.

We made it absolutely clear that our mission was to "shock people, in a good way." Unless you can shock people, you'll never gain new customers.

Since shocking people involves undermining what the customer expects, it requires determination. Take the Nintendo DS. At first, lots of people were confused. When we announced, "We're going to release a console that has two screens and a touch panel," most people must have thought, "Nintendo has gone off the deep end!"

In our eyes, staying the course meant that we had no future, but the average person probably thought it was a crazy idea.

The most important aspect of a job interview

I've always wondered why most interviews lead with the hardest questions. Why can't they lead with the easiest questions?

In my experience, there are two types of interviewers: those who make a person feel at ease in order to get a sense of who they really are and judge their candidacy accordingly, and those who believe an unrelaxed person, though unable to speak their mind, will reveal all kinds of things about themselves, like how sociable or strong they are.

I'm the first type. My belief is that the second type of interviewer is able to glimpse only a part of somebody's potential. Until you've let a person be themselves, the conversation hasn't really gotten started.

Maybe it's because I do so many interviews internally, but in my view, the most important aspect of the interview is starting in a way that makes it easy for the other person to respond.

When I'm speaking with somebody at the company for the first time, I begin by asking, "What made you decide to join Nintendo?" Because this is a question anyone can answer. Whatever the case may be, they'll have some kind of reason, and since the question is about them, there's no wrong answer. They can tell it like it is and speak the truth, giving you a glimpse of their true nature.

Conversely, if you ask them, "What's your take on Japan's decreasing birth rate and aging population?" or "What's going to happen to the US economy?" they may not be able to respond at all. And in that case, the interview has lost its meaning.

Apart from "What made you join the company," there's another question I like to ask: "Out of all the work you've done so far, what was the most interesting thing? And what was the most painful?"

This is all about them, too—making it easy to respond, and above all giving you a sense of who they are.

People who can accept constructive criticism

At the start of your career, it's only natural that you won't yet know about all kinds of things, but it's extremely important not to be embarrassed that you don't know.

If your primary motivation is to make the people working above you think, "Wow, this guy's so clever," they're going to see through you every time. And as if that wasn't bad enough, you'll come across as vain and leave a bad impression.

At the end of the day, what the company wants most from its new hires is someone who is happy to admit they don't know everything. But at the same time, they don't want you to ask your coworkers the same questions over and over.

New hires always seem to be divided between those who welcome criticism and those who don't—those people whose actions you can safely criticize and those you have to call out with the utmost care.

There's an enormous gap between the two. This vastly influences how much responsibility someone can take on, and how much they are able to absorb. The people who can take constructive criticism are capable of learning an incredible amount in a short period of time.

And when a person like this starts working at the office, it's a huge relief for everybody there.

What determines whether somebody can listen to criticism and take it in stride probably has to do with the purity of their motivations and behavior, and their lack of bad intentions. It's not about whether or not they can take a hit. Another key factor is that even when you criticize them, they recognize that it's not a personal attack. I think that having this shared trust is why you can safely give them negative feedback.

They may lack skills and know-how, but if they convey to you, "I'm receptive to what you have to say," you can give them clear instructions about what they're doing wrong or what needs their immediate attention, and trust they'll learn from what you're telling them.

Conversely, with the people you need to handle with the utmost care, you can sense this barrier around them, giving the signal, "Please don't go any further." Everybody has to walk on eggshells, scared that if they cross the line, they'll do this person irrevocable harm. If you can figure out what matters most to someone you can safely critique their work, but unless you have a sense of their values, you run the risk of unintentionally trampling over their feelings and priorities.

You become hesitant to show that you're upset or to offer criticism, scared of what might happen. This is why I think it's so important to be aware of whether a new hire will be receptive to feedback, and whether they will greet you with a smile on their face.

To put it simply, whenever possible, I want to assign work to those who actually want to do it. It's only natural. Who wants to ask someone to do something important if they don't seem to care?

Work is tough, full of unpleasant tasks. Some degree of perseverance is essential. Still, I suspect that whether or not a job is fun for someone depends a great deal on the breadth of their idea of what they're able to enjoy.

Depending on how you approach it, work can feel dull. But, if you're able to find the fun in discovering new things, almost everything you do can become interesting. This realization can be a major turning point in enjoying your job.

When a project is going well

In my experience, when a project is going well, it's not because an ideal leader has predicted every outcome, divvied up and allocated all the work, and brought it to fruition. Since the sort of work we do involves shocking and inspiring people, it's hard to take a practical approach, plan out everything beforehand, and break the work up into tasks.

So how do you know when a project is going well? When someone points to a gray area in the initial plan, then asks you "Hey, can I take care of this?" and follows through.

Projects where this keeps on happening tend to end up going well. On the other hand, when this phenomenon fails to occur, you might finish up all right, but things will feel a bit dysfunctional, which is never a good sign.

In that sense, making the Wii was an ideal experience, with people stepping up and saying "I see a problem here— how about I fix it?" more often than for any system up until then. There was something in the air making it happen.

Another factor was that the Wii development team had been debating what kind of a system the Wii should be since the earliest stages of the project. I think having a shared vision for the desired outcome is a major reason why the project was successful.

Once the whole team has a shared vision for the desired outcome, someone will be there to discover problems as they happen, or perhaps even before they happen, and attend to them organically. I guess that's what we call an ideal scenario.

The question of respecting others

No job is ever done alone. Someone else will always play a role. Companies provide a structure that allows for a variety of individuals to pool their efforts and accomplish huge tasks that could not be done alone.

If a manager could do everything on their own, they wouldn't have a company around them. Say you're the most reliable and have the most hands-on experience and the clearest understanding of the goal. If you can do it all yourself, you might as well, but if you do, the possibilities will be limited by your time and energy.

When people work together at a company, they allow their coworkers to take care of everything outside of their own responsibilities, letting go and bracing themselves for the results. As this arrangement increases in scale, it develops levels, broadening in scope. This is what we call a company.

When working this way, forging connections as we strive to achieve our objectives, respecting others—especially people who have different values and beliefs—becomes incredibly important.

There will always be people who see things differently than you. Perhaps to an unreasonable degree. Still, these people surely have their own reasons, their own history and values. Moreover, they're bound to be able to do things you can't do, and know things you don't know. This doesn't mean accepting everything they suggest, but respecting the fact that they have skills you lack, and are doing things that you can't do yourself. Whether or not you can maintain this respect will vastly influence how much fun and fulfillment you get out of a job.

In my case, I may be president of Nintendo, but I can't draw pictures or compose music. In terms of position, I may be an executive, with all the employees working under me, but each and every one of them is doing specialized tasks that I could never do myself.

I have nothing but the utmost respect for them. I've lived my life believing that people deserve respect.

What really firmed up this perspective was something Shigesato Itoi taught me in my early thirties. Itoi is over ten years older than me, but when I saw how much respect he showed toward people who could do things he didn't understand, I thought, "This guy is cool. I want to be like that."

Most importantly, though, I realized, "He's not doing anything exceptional, just showing honest admiration for people who can do things he can't do."

I'm not simply being moralistic. Treating the people you

meet on the job with respect makes your own work more fulfilling. That's all I'm trying to say.

On a side note, years ago, when I was a whole lot younger and felt a crazy sense of urgency, I used to tell myself, "I wish that I could clone myself three times over." Looking back, however, I recognize this thought was arrogant and narrow-minded. Our differences are what make each of us so valuable and give life meaning. I'm embarrassed that I ever thought this way.

These days, things have flipped. I take for granted that everyone has different strengths, and what I most want to learn about is what sets each person apart. Making space for this transforms relationships, opening up all kinds of possibilities. It's so exciting.

IWATA'S WORDS OF WISDOM
PART TWO

- Sometimes people have the potential to excel but get in their own way, telling themselves, "I'm bad at this, there's no way I can do this." Nobody in the whole world starts off their career thinking, "I have a knack for management." But time and again I've seen people who despise management, who say "I'm a creative, there's nothing else for me," change their point of view and realize, "Hey, teaching people stuff is pretty fun."

- These abilities had been there all along, but they simply hadn't noticed. When they finally realized, they were able to expand in ways they never would have dreamed of.

- Unless they have the self-confidence to announce, "I'm the best," engineers and artists never make any headway. Most programmers, too, believe their way of doing things to be superior. When these kinds of people join forces on a project, some conflict is unavoidable. Creativity, after all, is an expression of the ego.

- If everyone is dedicated and passionate, they all think, "I'm the one who's right." When everyone is going in different directions, what's the best way to conduct things? Soon after landing my first job, I became responsible for development. In a certain sense, this was great practice for my work as a manager.

- Being human means having potential. I see the role of the organization as making sure that everybody's latent potential is fostered as effectively as possible. The organization will squander its resources if energy is wasted on irrelevant tasks, but if you can direct that energy to the right place, you can exert incredible influence on the outside world.

- Someone might understand your explanation, but it takes a different kind of understanding for them to be able to relay the message to somebody else.

- Even when I'm vaguely aware of how tough it's going to be, my baseline assumption is, "We'll work it out." A leader has no other choice. The assumption that we'll be able to work it out makes the world go around. We all believe we need to work it out, myself included. When we made the Wii, I told my staff, "I want the console to be no thicker than three DVD cases." Knowing very well how difficult this would be, I pretended it was no big deal, though it must have been a challenge.

Still, this only works in moderation; sometimes you push the envelope, sometimes you don't. There needs to be a balance. If top management is always making unreasonable demands, the company can't operate.

- To reiterate, I firmly believe in the importance of setting goals, even when the goals are without precedent. If you simply keep piling on features, one after the next, things get crowded and the end result is bulky. But if you have a clear vision for what you want, you can say "Let's do it this way" and work your way backward from there. Granted, a president can't just say "Let's do it this way" once and expect everybody to share their vision. People need to hear the same thing over and over, but before long, something that you've said will stick. They'll realize, "Oh, that's what they mean." One person will get the gist, and then two more, and so on, until everybody realizes: "Nintendo set this as a goal. That's why we're here." That way everyone can share the same vision for the foreseeable future. Of course, this may mean sounding like a broken record for a while.

- The question is, when should you reach—that is, aim high? If it's in the stars, you'll be victorious, but if you reach too high and find out that your stars are crossed, you'll meet your ruin.

- The fact that the Nintendo DS was such a hit and the Wii was hugely popular all over the world comes down to a matter of luck. The one thing I can say with confidence, though, is that, as a company, Nintendo works incredibly hard to make good fortune come our way. Then again, the world is full of cases where people tried just as hard but luck wasn't on their side and things didn't work out.

- Even when your company is on top, you need to be ready to shake things up. When you have the greatest market share, you cannot lead the company in the same way as you would otherwise. But shaking things up is not enough. If you sense danger but you don't switch direction, things will speed up and spin out of control, which means you can't react too casually or you'll lose your chance. So, if I felt like the company was heading nowhere despite being on top, I think I'd change course drastically, to the point where people might even protest, saying, "We were on top. Why'd you have to do that? Why not play it by ear?" Sometimes, though, a totally different approach is unavoidable.

- The bigger an organization, the more important it is to decide, "All right! We're focusing on this now." Any company will have an endless list of pressing tasks, so if someone doesn't provide direction, the firm will gradually lose potency. That's why somebody like me, or Miyamoto, needs to step up to the plate and say, "Let's give this a try."

- What makes work so interesting is the chance to meet people driven by anger and people driven by happiness.

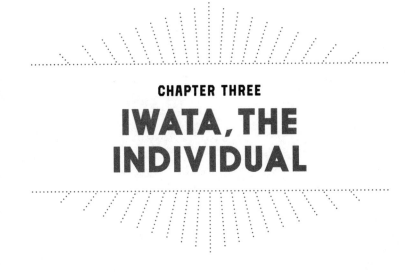

CHAPTER THREE

IWATA, THE INDIVIDUAL

A drive to understand why things happen

'm driven to understand why things happen. I can't be satisfied otherwise.

Inside of me, a voice is always asking questions: Why do things like this happen? What makes this person talk and act the way they do? How did the world wind up this way? I'm always searching for the reasons why things are the way they are.

As such, when presented with a fact, my first reaction is to come up with a hypothesis for why it happened. Once you have a hypothesis, you test it out, then come up with another. Pretty soon you can see further off, from angles that weren't available to you before.

I learned to see the world this way from Shigesato Itoi, who has a knack for seeing the future. More often than not, the things he likes catch on and become the next big hit. Working alongside him, I've seen this happen time and time again.

I'm always asking Itoi, "How did you know half a year out that this would be so popular?"

Without fail, Itoi answers the same way: "I don't predict the future. I simply notice the world starting to change a little before everybody else."

The first time I heard him say this, it made me wonder what it would take for me to be able to do this, too. So I started testing out different hypotheses, one after the other. Thanks to him, I think I'm far more capable than I was back then of sensing changes before other people have realized that they're happening.

Personally, I'm far more interested in what makes people happy than doing things the right way.

In my system of values, making the people around me happy and seeing them smile is absolutely paramount. There's a part of me that would do anything to make this happen.

But doing the right thing is easier said than done.

You might realize that somebody is making a mistake, but unless you can advise them in a way that they can readily accept and comprehend and fit into their point of view, your advice—right or not—is meaningless.

Lots of people will tell you that they know what's right. This is the cause of all kinds of conflicts. When two people with good intentions disagree, things can get ugly. That's because if you believe that your intentions are good, it feels as if you couldn't possibly be wrong. And as long as accepting the other person's point of view means negating your own core beliefs, there's no room for adjusting your position.

When this happens, the people who tell you that they're right neglect to ask themselves, "Why isn't my message getting across?"

Conversely, when both parties communicate effectively, it's safe to assume that one party has made a skillful compromise, allowing them to understand and sympathize with the other person.

The ability to find rewards

People have a way of sticking with some things and giving up on others.

For example, I think most people in Japan have probably told themselves, "I should really learn English." Nevertheless, the vast majority fail somewhere along the way.

To help make sense of this, I think I've found something we can turn to for a hint on whether we might be good at any given task. Interestingly, I gained this insight while developing video games.

Some video games are easy to stop playing, while others are strangely addictive. Two games can have the same high level of production quality, but a truly interesting game will break the mold. In my opinion, the same principle applies to whether we stick with a given activity.

What games and other activities have in common is our initial approach. At first, we give them all our energy. That could mean time, labor, or money. Once we've done our best, we have a response to what we've done, and whatever feeling we experience is our reward.

When the reward feels like it's greater than the energy and effort we've expended, we don't give up. But when the result of all our efforts is a disappointment, we tend to fail.

I think these conditions are essential to making games that people want to play, and this same logic helps to explain what makes or breaks a person's mission to learn English or the like.

For the same reason, if left to our own devices, we're going to get better at the things that we feel good at. As one example, a person who likes drawing is going to draw regardless of whether anybody asks them to, and people will praise them for that. As this cycle continues, they'll get better and better at drawing.

Take another example: early on, I knew almost nothing about computers, but as I put in the effort and learned about the way they worked, my increased understanding made things progressively more interesting.

The same applies to someone involved in product design or corporate planning. Watching the world, they'll try to create and release things that they find personally interesting. When other people like the things they've made, they get a boost of energy, and they do an even better job. The ability to establish such a cycle is what we might refer to, in these cases, as their talent.

Talent basically involves the ability to find rewards.

In my view, talent isn't about achieving results so much as deriving pleasure from the results that you've achieved.

When somebody has tapped into their stores of talent, the cycle of discovery and reward is up and running.

It's common for this cycle to shut down when a person is just inches away from reaching a reward. If this happens, sometimes all they need to hear is "Why not think of it this way?" or "I know you're feeling beat-up, but why not try a few more times?" and things might start going well again.

The instant we begin to feel that the rewards outweigh our efforts, a virtuous cycle starts up and keeps on going. It seems to me that whenever we can tell ourselves, "I think I'm good at this," the cycle of reward is in full swing.

Once we have one of these cycles going, our skill set begins to expand. One cycle of reward directs us to another, giving us a model for enjoying the rewards of new and different activities.

Something that we thought we were no good at begins to resonate, and soon we realize, "Hey, this is the same kind of thing." For example, I found myself discovering a considerable number of ways in which programming and corporate management overlap.

Unless we can uncover these connections, our skill set will never grow. Back when I focused exclusively on programming, I tried reading books on corporate organization and management, but because I couldn't make the connections, I was unable to retain what I was reading in any meaningful way. Sure, I may have been amassing knowledge, but knowledge on its own won't give you a sense of achievement. Nothing I read made me excited to try it out the next day. As a result, my reading failed to be rewarding.

If you force yourself to study things that have no bearing on the world around you, the material will have no way of sinking in. So, rather than waste your time, it makes far more sense to prioritize the things that you truly enjoy, whatever speaks to you.

How programming informs management style

Since programming depends on pure, uncompromising logic, a single contradiction will prevent the system from functioning properly. Machines don't make mistakes. All mistakes result from external forces. And so, when the system isn't working, the fault is clearly your own.

But the second programmers finish a program, they all try it out with the assumption "This is going to work like a charm." In reality, though, nothing ever works like a charm the first time. All the same, the moment they click Run, they have utterly convinced themselves that they have written every piece of code impeccably.

The world of programming runs on logic. If a program doesn't function properly, all the blame is on whoever programmed it.

In communicating with others, if I fail to get my point across, rather than blaming the other person, I will instead consider where I may have been at fault. When communication isn't going well, blaming others never helps. Instead, I tell myself, "They're not getting my message or seeing eye to eye with me because I'm not expressing myself as well as I could."

I'm sure this is the influence of programming. After all, when the system isn't working, your program is absolutely to blame!

So, when a conversation isn't going well, before I tell myself, "They just don't get it," I'll assume I was at fault. If things aren't going well, it's up to me to make a change. If I can find a way of doing things that works for them, I know that I can get my point across and win them over. To this day, when communication isn't working out, I ask myself where I went wrong. It's thanks to my background in programming that I can think this way.

But there are lots of other ways that programming informs management style. For example, when simplifying and resolving complicated problems that have several layers, my experience in programming is incredibly useful.

Analyzing problems is about breaking things down into discrete elements, while generating hypotheses for how to do things so that everything comes together. When programmers find a problem, they come up with a handful of hypotheses and weigh their merits, in a process that repeats daily.

And so, when I confront a complicated problem, my legs are ready to carry the load. After so many rounds of trial and error I trust the process, like someone who's been lifting weights every day.

If it makes sense for you, then go for it

When I'm up against something new or forced into a scenario where my usual way of doing things won't fly, I'll ask myself if there are any other decent options. Is there something better I could do instead? What would a different person do under the circumstances?

But regardless of whether I like it or not, once I'm convinced that I'm the best person for the job, I'm going to step up to the plate.

The tasks I've undertaken in the past were all cases where I thought I was the best person for the job. Even if I wasn't sure that I could pull it off, at the very least, I was absolutely certain that I was the best person to have a go at it.

This, too, is perhaps typical of a programmer.

My career has not been about what I like or dislike, or what I found challenging or unchallenging, but instead about what I thought made sense for me. Although it's not as if there haven't been all kinds of things I would just as soon have avoided!

To give a clear-cut example, I have never once enjoyed or thought that I was any good at being onstage and giving speeches. On top of that, since 2001 I've had to make speeches in English. Unfortunately, I didn't spend time living in America as a kid and was no good at English in high school.

But I've been doing this because I felt that it made sense for me to do it, rather than someone else. That conclusion gave me the resolve I needed. Since there was no way out of it, I figured I had better jump right in and take a positive approach.

In the same vein, there are loads of things that I'm not doing. For every task I tackle with resolve, there are tons of things that I stay out of because I don't actually need to be involved. That way, I can focus on the things that only I can do.

For the English speeches, I knew that someone had to do them. I'd delivered speeches in the period before I became the president of the company, so it wasn't unambiguously my responsibility as president.

But as it turned out, we had a big event in America, and someone had to get onstage and talk about the philosophy behind what Nintendo was up to.

Tapping Shigeru Miyamoto was an option, but in that case we would need to have him practice making speeches and presentations. My thought was that I'd rather have him spend his time creating more fun games than on that sort of thing. In which case, it was up to me. It was decided.

But what really matters is that this didn't turn out to simply be a chore. By taking this on, I discovered how fun it can be to learn to do something you couldn't do before.

It was tough, but at the same time I was able to enjoy it. As a result, I'm still making speeches in English, despite it being something I would never have imagined being good at.

The meaning of "Programmers should never say no"

A while back, I went on record saying "Programmers should never say no." When you're making games, if a programmer says, "That's impossible," it not only puts the brakes on a valuable idea but makes it harder for the next idea to come. If programmers only focus on things that are easy to program, they'll never break the mold and come up with fascinating ideas. Besides, through the process of trial and error, all kinds of things that seem impossible at first can wind up being a success.

This is why "no" is not a word that programmers should say lightly. I still believe this point to be essentially correct. But while I take responsibility for what I said, the statement has taken on a life of its own.

It's a matter of fact that when programmers say no to something, they close off possibilities, but not every aspect of development has limitless potential. Games are made under a limited set of restrictions. When something is legitimately impossible, you have no choice but to say so.

Sometimes an idea may be possible, but it's crucial that we factor in whether a given task will force you to sacrifice some other feature, or be incompatible with some other result.

I'd like for this to be a caveat to my idea "Programmers should never say no." It shouldn't be understood to mean "Programmers should never use the word impossible!"

Determine priorities and minimize regret

When the goal is making people happy, I'll gladly take on even the hardest problem and strategize solutions. Commenting on this tendency of mine, Shigesato Itoi jokingly called me "generous to a fault."

He has a point. If somebody is struggling or shows up with a problem, I get the itch to solve it. To be precise, if I'm presented with a problem, I can't help but seriously ask myself, "How would I handle this?" Not simply helping, but seriously considering things from their perspective.

And not because I particularly like the person, or because I feel sorry for them, but because I enjoy seeing people look pleased. And so, as a matter of principle, it doesn't matter who the person is, so long as they look pleased once we've resolved the problem.

Of course, there are only so many hours in the day, which means I'm forced to determine the total extent of time I can devote to each person and their problems. This poses something of a dilemma.

Especially these days, now that the emergence of the internet has eliminated such limitations as setting, distance, and physical space, we feel this dilemma more and more acutely.

When I asked myself what I could do about this, I finally decided to institute time restrictions. In the past, if I was at the headquarters in Kyoto and planning how to spend a day of work, I could only meet with people who were there in Kyoto. In which case, when I asked myself "Who should I see today?" I needed only to consider those in Kyoto with me. But now that the internet is in widespread use, we can regularly interact with people on the other side of the world.

The internet also has a way of broadening your motivations. In the past, it was possible to live without knowing there were people out there who we might be able to help, but today, we're able to see more situations where we might be of service. But this doesn't mean we've shed the limitations on the time at our disposal.

So, while our opportunities for interacting with others may have drastically increased, it's not as if we can engage with dozens or hundreds of people at once. As a result, it's become more difficult than ever to determine how to spend the hours of the day without regret.

This isn't simply about "working smart" and taking work more seriously. After all, the time you spend thinking about totally random stuff is never wasted.

Rather, it's more about deciding where to direct your limited supply of time and energy. On a deeper level, I think this is about doing what you were born to do.

Either way, spreading yourself thin will get you nowhere. Same goes for companies. If you let the masses dictate your decision-making, you're forced to cast a wide net, and you won't be able to give individual projects the attention they deserve. As a result, the work lacks depth, and above all, has no secondary gains.

The best bet, both on the individual level and the corporate level, is to take stock of your abilities and assign priority to minimize regret. Regret is part of life, but it's something we would all rather avoid. If we can even slightly dial back how often we tell ourselves, "I wish I'd done things differently," I think we'd be a whole lot happier.

IWATA'S WORDS OF WISDOM
PART THREE

- In a completely different environment, I think I would surrender to my curiosity. I'm the sort of person who, if left to his own devices, will find something interesting to do and, when I'm ready, will share what I've made with those around me. If they like it, I couldn't be happier.

- I've been thinking: people waste time worrying about problems that can't be solved by worrying. If worrying would solve the problem, then I'd say go ahead and worry, but somehow we can't stop ourselves even when worrying solves nothing and leaves us empty-handed.

- You can be younger than me, with fewer years at the company and less experience, but if you're able to write a shorter, faster program, you don't need me to tell you that it's good. A program that does the same thing, except shorter and faster… There's something great about that. How could I not tip my hat to you and learn from your example? If someone can do something that I can't, regardless of whether I like or dislike their personality, I'll still admire their ability. And if that makes me impartial, I suppose I am.

- Picture yourself at restaurant. A customer looks at their food and says it's "too much." When a person says "too much," what makes them see things that way? At the root, the problem isn't about there being too much, but rather about the food being unappealing. Plenty of times, things can look excessive when there really isn't too much there. If you overlook the unappealing aspect, and simply reduce the portion, it won't make any difference. If the problem is about it being unappealing, you need to fix the unappealing thing. At first glance, the idea of scaling back because it was too much may seem like a solution, but it solves nothing.

- When I'm really hooked on something, as long as I can figure out what got me hooked, I can take that process and apply it elsewhere as a way of drumming up interest.

- When you make things for a living, your daily work is divided between things that only human beings can do and things a machine may as well do instead. This is why I'm interested, from an early stage, in creating frameworks for automating the things a machine may as well do instead. I've always been easily bored by menial labor. I want to have fun and focus on the things that I enjoy. I can't imagine spending each and every day doing the same menial tasks over and over— but I'd hate to put that work on someone else.

- "Creating things that people can enjoy regardless of age, gender, or background," the stance I take when carrying out the mission of Nintendo, has certain things in common with ideas like "The simpler the functionality, the better" or "Things should be easy to use" or "When a customer has too many choices, they get confused," the corporate philosophy of Apple—or more specifically the value system of Steve Jobs. On the other hand, Apple clearly specializes in technology, while Nintendo focuses on entertainment. This results in massive differences in priority. Make no mistake, I would without hesitation choose to make a product sturdier over making it 0.5 millimeters thinner. And I don't think Apple needs to subject the iPod to the sort of endurance testing where it's dropped repeatedly from the height of a bicycle basket. If Apple and Nintendo have something in common, it's increasing appeal through simplification. As you develop an idea, things begin to simplify. But on the whole, we're different, because of differences in priority.

- When I give a speech or a lecture, I prepare all of my notes myself. Even for presentations. Unless I make my own materials, I can't be satisfied.

CHAPTER FOUR

THE PEOPLE IWATA BELIEVES IN

Good ideas solve multiple problems in a flash

"**A** good idea is something that solves multiple problems in a flash." This is something that Shigeru Miyamoto taught me at Nintendo about making games. For him, the phrase functions as a kind of creed of game design, but I see the idea as extending beyond games and being universally applicable.

When you're making something, whatever it may be, you're always going to have the problem of "if I do this, I can't do that."

Up against a given problem, you'll have some choices that will make things better and others that will make things worse, but when designing a product, you'll never find yourself in the ideal circumstance of having just one problem to solve. It's more likely you'll have problems everywhere you look! This doesn't apply just to products, but to organizations and interpersonal relationships as well.

Faced with a slew of problems, you might pick one, decide, "Okay, things will work great if I address this," and make some kind of an improvement—but it won't translate into overall progress. Once you're done fixing the problem, another one is sure to pop up in its place, and something that was working fine before won't work anymore.

At brainstorming meetings, where people talk about how to tackle problems, there will always be a variety of ideas, but most of them will only solve one problem at a time, leaving the other problems unattended to. In that case, you'll only ever progress in proportion to your level of exertion.

When it comes to games, most of the time the concern is that they won't be interesting enough. A game that hooks players in all kinds of ways will capture their attention and be satisfying. Trouble is, you can only allocate so much time and personnel to a given project. With finite resources, telling people "more is better" will never solve your problems.

However, once in a while, you'll do this one thing that will solve a problem here, but also something over there, and even things you hadn't realized would be problems.

Shigeru Miyamoto is always looking for that one thing, pushing himself and relentlessly asking, "What is it? What is it?"

Back when I was president of HAL Laboratory, Miyamoto would call me up occasionally, and what do you think was the first thing he would say?

"I got it, Iwata."

When Miyamoto said, "I got it," he meant he had an idea for the game that we were making together, but specifically, he meant, "This idea will take out three or four of the big problems that are bugging us."

A single breakthrough that will make this thing better, and that thing better. This is the definition of a good idea, and having one will move the project forward, closer to your goal.

Miyamoto believes that making these discoveries is the responsibility of anyone with the title of director.

Taking this advice to heart, I see no way that it could only work for games. The world is full of situations where "if I do this, I can't do that." We call this sort of thing a trade-off, and everyone in the entire world is making trade-offs every day.

Things will get better if we spend more. Things will get better with more help. If we give this thing more time, we'll do a much better job. These trade-offs are obvious, but if you only think within that framework, you'll move along at the same pace as everybody else and will lack a competitive edge.

However, if you can find a way of combining your resources to great effect, especially in novel ways that have been overlooked, value compounds. Arriving at the root cause of a problematic situation, you'll find that several problems that appeared to have been independent issues are in fact connected at a common source, so a single measured change will affect various seemingly unconnected areas, solving multiple problems simultaneously.

When Shigeru Miyamoto calls me up and says, "I got it," he means that he's had an idea that will eliminate a bunch of problems in one go, and that he now has a view of the big picture.

What Miyamoto sees over your shoulder

When I was starting out as a game developer, if my creations didn't sell, I used to ask myself, "Why aren't they selling?"

Not to brag, but I don't think they were lacking technical distinction. Yet they weren't selling. Meanwhile, the games that Shigeru Miyamoto made were selling several times, or even several dozen times, as well as the games I had been working on. Despite the fact that mine, in terms of programming, were up to snuff.

I wanted my games to be popular. Just like his.

Miyamoto makes his games by taking leaps of faith, deciding that "if we do this, here's what we can expect," and in that sense he has a much higher batting average than most, but he is not omnipotent, and makes his fair share of mistakes.

But how does he fix them?

By snatching up some person in the company who has never touched the game. He pulls them from their desk, without explanation, hands them a controller, and says "All right, play."

He's been doing this since he was in middle management, long before he became the internationally renowned game designer his is today.

Since the early days, Miyamoto has been spiriting away these unassuming employees and sitting them down with a controller. Telling them "Go on, play" and watching from behind without further explanation. I like to call this "what Miyamoto sees over your shoulder."

I didn't understand how crucial this was until we started working together. Once we did, I realized, "Oh, of course."

A person who makes games can't sit down with everyone who buys them and explain, "Here's how I designed things. Here's how to play." Obviously that would be impossible. The product needs to be self-explanatory.

However, the product is incapable of conveying every single little detail. Some things are going to be lost. Players will wind up confused by things the game designers have never considered.

This is what Miyamoto looks for when he watches "over your shoulder."

When you watch somebody playing a game that they know nothing about, you learn heaps of things about what parts are confusing, or which tricks they miss completely, or the spots where they miss steps that make things harder later. This gives you an idea of how a player reacts when they have no prior knowledge of the game.

Miyamoto rates his level of accomplishment as a game designer on these terms, believing that if a customer fails to understand what to do, he has failed.

Simply put, it's all about the customer's point of view, and Miyamoto has a way of getting there extremely early in the process. Meanwhile, I was mostly interested in how cool my programs were but had failed to consider how actual players might receive them.

Lots of designers talk like I did back in the day, saying things like "Well, I think this is pretty cool," speaking on behalf of the entire gaming population. What's really needed is to address the reality of how players react, and ask the question "Why is that?" and finally "What can we do to get to the root of the problem?" But all too often people say, "I see it differently!" They hopelessly confuse theory and reality and force their opinions on others.

What sets Miyamoto apart is that despite being extremely stubborn when it comes to his designs, he'll watch a person play a game for the first time with extreme equanimity. He'll see how they react, and if he decides that they're missing the point, he'll go back to the drawing board and try a fresh approach.

One day he'll be looking at this thing up close, then suddenly he'll be looking at it from an incredible distance and reworking things. It's as if one second he's using a magnifying glass, and the next instant he's looking down from ten thousand feet overhead.

Usually, when people spend a lot of time looking at something, they get closer and closer and lock themselves into a particular way of seeing.

I think the sort of ideas that Miyamoto talks about, ideas that can solve multiple problems in one go, become harder to find the closer you examine things. The sort of details you won't notice unless you change your point of view are lost on the average person.

Because Miyamoto is so ready to change up his perspective, he's able to arrive at actual solutions rather than implementing stopgap measures that save one life by sacrificing another.

I think most people out there think of Miyamoto as an artist—something of a genius, who puts stock in inspiration and thinks with the right side of his brain, coming up with unlikely observations one after another, as if guided by divine inspiration.

But that's not the case. Miyamoto is an extremely logical person. But that's not all. His mind is capable of both extraordinarily logical, left-brained considerations and the sort of speeding-bullet thinking you might hear from someone who has pursued a career in the arts. I hate to say it, but I envy him.

I'm not saying that I'm altogether without right-brained insights or abilities. But once I started working with Miyamoto and made the acquaintance of Shigesato Itoi, I wasn't about to try competing with them. The odds are stacked against me!

As a general rule, I'd rather play to my strengths than do something that I'm bad at.

Miyamoto's keen understanding of computers

Though I don't think Shigeru Miyamoto has ever made a formal study of computers or programming, he's had his hand in game design since the early days, when computers were incredibly simple, and so he has a firm grasp of the computer as a tool for realizing the things he wants to do.

Granted, he may lack the specialized knowledge of how exactly one might go about writing a program on a computer, but his comprehension of what computers are good at—and bad at, for that matter—is absolutely spot-on.

So, if a programmer tells him, "We can't do that," rather than responding, "You'll figure it out," he asks them, "How are things set up now?" Once the programmer has explained the setup, he'll say, "If you can leverage your setup this way, can't you make this other thing work?" To which they'll say, "In that case, yeah."

Our experience with making *Pikmin* demonstrates this perfectly. The setup and the individual movements of that game are simple. Putting everything together was another story, however. At the most basic level, computers depend on simple commands, but these simple things can be combined and processed into elaborate designs. That's what makes programming fun, but also difficult.

Miyamoto may not be involved in the nuts and bolts of programming, but he has a thorough understanding of how the fundamental parts take shape.

You could say his role is understanding and discussing principles and functionalities. As a result, even without specialized knowledge, he's able to engage with programmers. This allows him to put himself in the shoes of a programmer who is convinced that something can't be done and propose an alternative.

This kind of game designer is something of a rarity.

There are many people who throw solutions at a problem from all different angles. When our games take this kind of an approach, regardless of whether Miyamoto is involved, they achieve an extremely high production quality, and if you zoom in on the individual details, you'll find the finished product to be stunning.

However, this sort of thing is not what determines the reception of a game.

Two ways of resuscitating *EarthBound*

When development for *EarthBound* (released as *Mother 2* in Japan) was in shambles, I was called in to save the sinking ship. At the time, I was both the president of HAL Laboratory and one of its programmers.

I tended to agree that the game was not heading in the right direction. So I came right out and said to Shigesato Itoi, "The way it is, I don't think it will work."

And I added this: "If you'd like, I'd be happy to lend a hand, but I see two ways of going forward."

From there, I said something that has become the stuff of legend among gaming fans:

"Working with what we have, it would take two years to fix things up. If you don't mind starting from scratch, we could be done in half a year."

In the end, we wound up remaking the game from scratch, but I could have gone about things either way, and I think the game would have worked out regardless.

If I had been asked to determine the best course of action, I think I probably would have said, "Let's start from scratch." Still, I had been called in after the fact to get the project on its feet again, and I was ready to go with the flow.

How could I show up out of nowhere and tell all these people who had worked so hard, "All right! We're starting over?" Everyone would have dragged their feet. When the mood in the workplace sours, it can make a good thing fall apart. Therefore, I determined the right thing to do was to present the two possible options and let those involved make the decision.

From start to finish, *EarthBound* was in development for almost five whole years—the first four years without me, and the last year with me helping out.

I may have reorganized the game from scratch, but the constituent elements had come into being during the four years when I wasn't around. The graphics were done, and the story and soundtrack were essentially complete. So the materials were basically in place.

The first time I visited the team, everyone's files were more or less in order. I said to them, "I'll play around with what we have," and I went back with the project in its current state. About a month later, I showed Shigesato Itoi and his team a revised version, with the scrolling map and everything.

Were they surprised! In fact, they were all freaking out so much I honestly felt confused. I was like, "Guys, I barely did anything." That's how bogged down the project was.

Approximately six months later, *EarthBound* had finally come together, to the point where we could actually play around with it. From there, we made another pass to polish things, spending six more months working out the kinks, until it was finally complete.

It may appear as if everything happened in the one year I was involved, but we were only able to get *EarthBound* that far in a year's time because of the four years of work that had already been completed. A game like that, with such a variety of interesting detail and character, could never result from a yearlong sprint. The four years up until development hit an impasse were absolutely not in vain. *EarthBound* brims with the spirit of experimentation that guided all of those who toiled over its design.

EarthBound and expanding the gaming population

The *Mother* series has maintained a cult following for years, and people often point to these games as favorites. Interestingly, the things that people remember fondly about the games vary widely.

Some people love the music, while others love the writing. Fans have so many different favorite parts. I've heard people talk about how one part made them cry, and others mention how the sound that Master Belch made grossed them out. Players have shared a whole range of poignant experiences, from being moved to tears to cracking up because of how goofy it was.

When you listen to somebody else's reminiscences, you will often find yourself agreeing with them, even though your experiences may differ. And when you mention your own favorite parts, you're bound to hear assenting voices all around. People remember so many different aspects of the game.

What makes the *Mother* games so special? I think it has to do with the role Shigesato Itoi played. Nobody making games today is quite like Shigesato Itoi, and *Mother* remains without parallel in the world of games.

There was a time when Shigesato Itoi was totally obsessed with video games, and in that sense he's truly a gamer at heart. At the same time, he had a variety of experiences that the average game designer hadn't, and I think these two aspects combined to form a unique individual.

Mother takes the large-scale format typical of Japanese RPGs, so in that sense it isn't necessarily special. Still, the overall effect is a game unlike almost any other. I think this is the cumulative result of all the aspects of the gaming experience—the fun parts, sad parts, outlandish parts, and goofy parts that Shigesato Itoi packed into the game. There really isn't anything else like it out there.

"Grown-ups, kids, the girl next door." That's the copy Shigesato Itoi wrote for *EarthBound*. Joining *EarthBound* in its final stages and becoming acquainted with Shigesato Itoi, I took this message to heart and bore it in mind when I pledged, after becoming the president of Nintendo, to expand the gaming population. After all, what's expanding the gaming population if not including "grown-ups, kids, and the girl next door?"

If you play *EarthBound* for long enough, the game is set up so that the father character will call you up and say, "Don't you think it would be a good idea if you took a break?" This is a concept that we carried over to the Wii. Without the precedent of these calls from dad every two hours, the Wii feature that keeps track of your total hours of game-play would not exist.

As you can see, I not only took part in the development of *EarthBound* but derived considerable inspiration from the work, which stands out from the rest as a game that is truly unique.

How I described my view of work to Shigesato Itoi

I have a conversation with Shigesato Itoi seared into my memory. This happened just after development of *EarthBound* was finished, when I asked him if he'd be willing to serve as a consultant for HAL Laboratory, where I was working at the time, and was visiting his office to discuss the possibility.

On that occasion, for whatever the reason, I shared my work philosophy with him. And you know what? I don't think that what I told him then has changed, all these years later.

"It makes me really happy when people enjoy my work. This could mean gamers, or maybe friends, or maybe the companies we work with, but what interests me is helping people to enjoy themselves. Seeing the people around me looking pleased is what keeps me going." That's the gist of what I said.

Looking back, I'm not sure what possessed me to be so open with somebody I'd known for just over a year and wasn't especially close to.

I mean, it wouldn't be so crazy to say this kind of thing to an old friend, but I was talking like this guy had been my mentor for twenty years at least—because he made me feel that way.

What I'll truly never forget is how Itoi said to me, once I had finished talking, "I feel the same." That's when I realized, "Oh, that's what made this work. We approach so many things in entirely different ways, have totally different personalities, and have taken different paths, but in a fascinating case of synchronicity, we have the same work philosophy."

What's more, I was convinced that Itoi and I had become extremely close already. I think the reason we've worked together all these years is that the things that matter most to us are incredibly similar. It's all because the first time I shared my work philosophy, he told me he felt the same, and said it from the heart. That's why we're still working together.

To this day, feeling useful to others and knowing somebody enjoys my work is what gets me through the day. I genuinely look forward to reading customer surveys, and still get super excited when somebody praises a product or makes it clear how much they're enjoying it.

I think this speaks directly to the reason why I work, and even the reason why I'm on this earth. Without that kind of boost, even a wealth of energy will gradually expend itself.

But when I see the smiling faces of our fans, or hear my friends say "Thanks," it replenishes my stores. For everyone working at Nintendo, it lifts our spirits and keeps us going when we see our customers smile.

The lessons of Hiroshi Yamauchi

Over the course of the five years that it took me to rebuild HAL Laboratory, which were the years before I started working for Nintendo, I had the opportunity two or three times a year to sit down with Hiroshi Yamauchi, the president of Nintendo at the time. Shigesato Itoi was also there, and sometimes Shigeru Miyamoto would join us.

I'm still not sure what Hiroshi Yamauchi had in mind when he set up those meetings, but I know they were valuable lessons for me. He must have known we were an eager audience. Despite being extremely busy, he set aside his valuable time to enthusiastically share his thoughts. President Yamauchi was infamous for never smiling, but when he spoke with us, he always grinned like crazy.

Looking back, it's almost like we were in school—a school of management. What is "fun"? What is "software"? What does Nintendo value as a company? What should Nintendo strive to do, and to avoid?

Yamauchi used to tell us, "If Nintendo tries to fight, it's gonna lose. Don't waste your energy on fighting." In today's business parlance, this translates into the idea of "blue ocean strategies."

Hiroshi Yamauchi realized at a very early date that when you're creating a new piece of hardware, if all it does is re-package the same old gaming experience, it won't actually feel new, and the gaming population won't expand. It doesn't matter if it's a handheld console or a home console. If you make the same old thing, it won't have character. And if it lacks character, all you do is add to the competition.

Yamauchi liked to discuss things in terms of natural inclinations. At the root, this overlaps with the focus on ability so central to my approach to managing the company, where people play to their strengths. I was young back then, and suspected that it wasn't worth the effort to put so much weight behind people's natural inclinations, but in hindsight, I recognize that he had touched upon an essential truth.

Thereafter, I received all kinds of lessons from Yamauchi. Time and again, he told us, "Don't do anything that's been done before."

I remember one iconic episode where he recommended that we "make a game console that has two screens," which eventually led to the Nintendo DS. In the end, the system literally wound up having two screens, but at the time, I thought it was a metaphorical way of saying that we should "make something totally unlike anything that's come before." I figured the essential point was to not do anything that had been done before.

And so, Yamauchi's "two screens" idea had been a topic of interest for me and Miyamoto since long before we started working on the DS. Then one day we realized how fun it would be if we combined touch screen capabilities with a two-screen handheld console, and in one of those eureka moments, we had a practical idea of how to move forward.

I remember that moment so clearly. We were talking in the parking lot of an Italian restaurant near the office, where Miyamoto and I like to go for lunch, and suddenly it hit me. "Hah! I've got it."

Just goes to show how Yamauchi's lessons have lived on inside of me. I can't tell you how many times he told us, "Don't do anything that's been done before." That said, it's not like you immediately come up with an unprecedented idea, so you have to say "I'll keep that in mind" and let it be a guiding principle. Yamauchi was a man of unwavering conviction, and he consistently instilled in us the same message. Over time, it started rubbing off on us. At this point, it's become a part of me, to the point where I can hear myself repeating him. Though perhaps I'm a bit more ... soft-spoken.

Anyway, I'll never forget the things that Yamauchi taught us. After all, what he did with Nintendo as a company makes him a miracle worker, the sort of person whose words demand respect. If I hear someone saying "Oh no, that again..." about something that he used to say, I give it to them straight: "The Nintendo of today is nothing short of a miracle."

IWATA'S WORDS OF WISDOM
PART FOUR

- When Shigesato Itoi shares his thoughts, it's always something I would never think of, always a point of view I would have missed. He's invariably throwing curveballs, things I never saw coming. Still, though, he makes sure to throw them easily so I can catch them. There hasn't been a single one I've failed to catch. But his pitching style is always new, which keeps things incredibly interesting.

- The legacy that Yamauchi left Nintendo is enormous. Without his contribution, Nintendo would not be a what it is today. The reason the Nintendo DS has two screens, for example, is that Yamauchi championed the idea so consistently. The demand to make something with two screens had been with us for a while, a persistent source of motivation, to the point where Miyamoto and I basically reverse engineered the thing, asking ourselves "What are the possibilities for two screens?" and brainstorming from there. As a result, we wound up with the idea of using one of the screens as a touch screen. Without Yamauchi's enthusiasm, the Nintendo DS would not have taken shape this way.

- Coming up with fascinating frameworks time and time again is one of Miyamoto's great achievements. Miyamoto can pick up a piece of software under development and instantly recognize things the rest of us have missed. This has happened countless times. I'm not so sure he does it consciously, but I always wish I could have beat him to the punch!

- Oftentimes, when the "ship's about to leave," we wind up having to retool the molds because of our old pal Miyamoto. These slight adjustments to the hardware pop up every time.

- So much of what I know about making games I learned from Miyamoto. Or perhaps not so much learned as stole. I've been watching and learning since my days at HAL Laboratory. Frankly, I spent years watching Nintendo with eyes wide open, trying to figure out what makes Miyamoto so perpetually successful. Today, as fate would have it, I'm making things at the same company as him, and honestly, it's as much fun as its sounds.

- One of the most interesting things about the way Miyamoto forms ideas is how he works from functionality.

Rather than arbitrarily adding characters to a story, he starts off with a functional premise such as "This will be boring unless there's someone here." This mode of thinking suggests the mind of somebody well versed in industrial design. As one example, Miyamoto's idea, way back when, to have Mario ride on Yoshi's back in *Super Mario World* sprang from a place of functionality. To be specific, the Super Famicom system did not allow for us to display a large number of sprites (a technical method for displaying graphical objects on the screen) in a row. Yoshi is shaped the way he is in order to limit the number of sprites in a row when Mario is riding him. If you look at the diagrams for Yoshi, it's easy to see that he was designed purely from a place of functionality. We made Yoshi a dinosaur not because we wanted Mario to ride a dinosaur, but because the space we had, in terms of functionality, was shaped much like a dinosaur.

- Miyamoto ascribes a great deal of importance to the functionality of the first part of a game. As a result, his sense of what the player needs to be told is extraordinarily clear, which allows for him to make specific observations like "We need more of this" or "You have to make the sequence go this way." A game's designers, by virtue of working on a project from the start, will naturally become insensitive to where a person playing for the first time will get lost, and as development comes to a close, the blind spots become immense.

That's where Miyamoto comes in. I think this act of "knocking down the house of cards" is actually in some ways unavoidable.

- Miyamoto has a startling ability to point out faults while allowing the material at hand to be salvaged. This never fails to leave me feeling impressed. Those inclined to "knock down the house of cards" are often overeager to scrap everything, but Miyamoto firmly believes that it would be a waste to throw it all away. If we're left with material we can't use, he'll make a mental note and later on propose we add it in elsewhere. This goes against what comes to mind when you hear "knocking down the house of cards."

- When Miyamoto hears someone state a reason something is impossible, he counters with the question, "What would it take to make it possible?" And from there he establishes the necessary conditions. This is about "cornering the opponent and jabbing at the weak points they can't block."

- People all over the world seem to think of Miyamoto as being surrounded by a crowd of famous characters, which he can pick from readily. As if all he had to do, when making a game, was drop in one of these famous characters and immediately win the world's attention. People like me, who have known Miyamoto since the old days, know this isn't actually the way it is. In the beginning, Mario was called "Jumpman," but long before anybody knew the name "Mario," Miyamoto had been working on his character, just like he had for Donkey Kong, and for Link in *Zelda*, and for the Pikmin. It all starts with a character, but characters don't attract attention on their own. They result from a continuous investigation of their traits, until finally they become extravagant or can hold their own for all their simplicity. We call this "Miyamoto Magic," but if you asked Miyamoto, he's merely using common sense and working through things carefully.

- One way of defining a genius is "a person who can endlessly continue doing things that other people might dislike or easily grow tired of and be unable to continue." I think that's what we mean when we say "genius"—not giving up on your ideas, letting them have all the space they need. It may be exhausting, or it may perhaps be rewarding, but in any case it certainly isn't easy. For a person who can do these things, however, it also isn't torture. Those who think of it as torture will never surpass those who don't see it as torture. That's the essence of genius. Those who can persevere without thinking that they're suffering, and thereby discover valuable things, are able to derive happiness from that alone.

- I count myself as Shigeru Miyamoto's number one follower in all the world.

CHAPTER FIVE

THE GAMES IWATA STRIVES TO MAKE

The game console we envisioned

As early game consoles gained popularity, family members began to want their own personal televisions. In that sense, the number of televisions per household increased in direct proportion with the popularity of video games. Indeed, the period when families started owning multiple televisions overlaps precisely with the Famicom and the Super Famicom becoming part of daily life.

The advent of digital broadcasting brought massive flat-screen televisions, however, making it common once again for families to have one big TV in the living room.

The Wii was designed precisely for use with bigger televisions of this kind. Large flat-screen TVs meant a little bit more open floor space, allowing everyone to move their bodies and play around. In our humble opinion, this was a breakthrough.

With a game console, it's not only about what the thing can do, but the various conditions under which the gameplay will occur.

It may sound obvious, but a game console will have all kinds of players. With so many people approaching a product from different points of view, what you felt was a product with a specific vision inevitably turns out to be interpreted in many different ways.

In the automotive industry, these tastes are accommodated by a wide lineup of cars, with different types for different personalities, but this isn't how Nintendo makes game consoles.

At one extreme, we are aiming for something that's enticing from every angle, but as you try to check off all the boxes, you start debating stuff like "What are people who don't have internet supposed to do?" and poking fun at your ideas just as they come together. You want to consider things from a variety of angles and fill in the gaps, while keeping within the bounds of possibility.

Back then, we were envisioning a kind of video game that people could pick up on any given day. Our ideal wasn't a console people would play daily, but one that blended readily with daily life.

Back when video games broke into the mainstream, there were lots of people who had no interest in playing them and never touched a game console. I wanted these kinds of people to see the device as not only unobtrusive, but in fact beneficial to their lives. And if, as a result of these games becoming more readily accessible, the number of people who recognized the fun of video games suddenly increased, what could be better?

The original idea behind video games was to use the television as an interface for play, but in the future, our definition of play is certain to expand tremendously.

Lots of people flick on the television without any thought the second they get home. The reason they turn on the television even when they don't have any specific show in mind is the confidence that once they're home, as long as they press the power button on the remote, something will happen, which feels better than doing nothing. I think this is the main reason why television assumed such a presence in our lives.

I can't think of anything more fun than game consoles taking on a similar presence in our daily routine. Not to brag, but as long as you switch on the console, you're certain to enjoy yourself. That said, I recognize that turning on a video game is easier said than done.

A store can sell the finest products, but only if the customers show up. In the same way, unless people are turning on the console, even the most entertaining games will go unplayed. Moreover, there are loads of enjoyable games out there that people would love playing, if they only knew that they existed. For the most part, customers take a passive stance, which means not actively seeking out new games to play. Part of our job is to make sure these people know these interesting games exist.

In the history of video games, there have been times where people dragged their game consoles out of the closet only when a new *Dragon Quest* or *Mario* game came out, but otherwise kept it unplugged from the TV. Which meant a primary goal was to get people to keep their consoles plugged in. The next step was developing a system that people would turn on every day. That's how I saw it.

Creating a platform for play

In my opinion, the strength of interactive entertainment, epitomized by video games, is that you look back ten or fifteen years after the fact and remember playing them. Granted, literature and movies can also leave a strong impression, but even when the memory is strong, you're often unable to so much as summarize the plot. However, because video games are interactive, allowing you to steer the action, they stimulate the brain in a peculiar and extremely powerful way.

In that sense, if a form of entertainment has an interactive element, I believe it shouldn't be restricted by the boundaries of traditional video games. Unless games can explore genres and themes that have been overlooked, we can't expect the actual number of people who enjoy them to increase. Hence our attempt, with the Nintendo DS, to expand the gaming population by proactively incorporating themes that had not been explored by the games of the past.

I think the people of the world today have experienced far too many different things for us to be able to create games where the experience is fully formed without your input and the end result is satisfying. As you experience more and more different things, the desire for novel forms of entertainment grows ever stronger. If we tried to account for all these wants and needs, a game console would never come together.

For this very reason, we've created hardware that provides a structural framework for play so that different people can interpret the games in their own way and share their experiences with others. If the hardware has been engineered to have a robust framework, prompting a variety of gameplay, it greatly influences the potential for the system down the line. In that sense, I think that firmly establishing a promising foundation early on is among the most crucial aspects of designing a gaming platform.

I think what sets our game consoles apart is that they go beyond high performance by promising a variety of gameplay possibilities and consistently delivering on their promises. At the same time, we don't simply view our games in terms of big-picture concepts, but talk about them like the fans we are, telling each other, "That game is awesome! Can't wait until it comes out." To this day, we strive to make games that we find genuinely exciting.

What starts as an absurdity can still bear fruit

In developing the Wii, I asked myself repeatedly, "what can we do to prevent video games from being seen as an intrusion on family life?" This led to the hypothesis, or perhaps the absurd proposition, of a feature that would allow parents to set a daily time limit for gaming—say one hour per day— where the console would physically shut off after one hour of gameplay.

What could possess the president of a video game company to think such things?

Obviously, all your data would be saved before it happened. I'll admit this feature was a bit aggressive, but all the same ... I was dead serious. I mean, I knew it was an awful proposition. Still, though, I was convinced that in the absence of a controversial proposition, we would never come up with anything new. At the very least, I knew that starting a debate from such an angle would prove valuable.

And let me tell you, the debate was heated.

Some argued this was unacceptable, while others said that such extremes were necessary to change the minds of mothers worried about how much time their children spent gaming. We debated whether it was technologically possible, investigating the particulars of how to save all of the data after one hour elapsed, and what would happen when you picked up the game the next day.

In the end, it was made thoroughly apparent to me just how difficult this would be, and that there were other, better options for fulfilling our objective that would not require us to forcibly shut off the power, so this feature fell by the wayside.

The result of our debate was the "play history" functionality, which allows everyone to see which games you've played, and for how long. Unlike the extreme measure of killing the power, which gave you no choice but to play one hour per day, the "play history" encourages a dialogue between kids and their parents that promotes accountability.

As first proposed, the idea was absurd, but the ensuing process of debate was not in vain. Though I'll admit it caused some people stress.

The shutoff feature never came to be, but one idea that we retained was not running the fan at night. Since we envisioned the Wii as a "sleepless machine" that would stay on twenty-four hours a day, this point was nonnegotiable. If the fan stayed running all night, your mother might think you'd left it on again and pull the plug.

The hazards of staying the course

I'm not so naive as to have optimistically imagined that the Nintendo DS would be such a hit, or that it would become a cultural phenomenon that spread across the world to Europe and America. Or that the same would happen with our release of the Wii.

It's reasonable to worry about how people will assess the value of something that is unlike anything that's come before. Ironically, this is the very thing that pushes me to get our message across.

Attempting things that nobody has done before not only means having no guarantee of success—it also means you can't be cavalier and expect minimal results. I guess sometimes you just need to take the plunge.

Early in development, there are so many unknowns: concerns about technology, a lack of a concrete image for the goal, an unclear course of action. After all, taking a different path than others is truly terrifying. On the one hand, society revolves around the principle of strength in numbers, but we often have no choice but to find our own way. Honoring people for being different is part of Nintendo's company culture, but being different comes in a huge range of shapes and sizes, and is particularly frightening when you're moving in the opposite direction from everyone else.

Though speaking personally, I think nothing is more hazardous than staying the course.

Nobody can say for sure when to make a change. When Nintendo takes a different tack, there's no telling whether it will take one year, or two, or three, or even five for people to catch on.

But staying the course means not having a future.

If you maintain the status quo, you wind up fighting for survival, and gradually your fan base disappears. That's the one direction I'm always trying to avoid.

There's always the question of how far you can shift and still have people understand and follow along. However, forging straight ahead will get you nowhere. I recognized that plugging away down a path that had no future, toward oblivion, would mean all of our effort was in vain, and knowing this steeled my resolve.

As long as we could expand the gaming population, we would have a future. Of that much, I was certain.

If I could turn back time, I'd make it the same

I think that the secret of controller design at Nintendo is that development of the controller, on the hardware side, is linked with the development of the corresponding software from an early stage.

In practice, this means that once the software team receives a controller idea from the hardware side, they set about making prototype games, and report their findings back to hardware. This accumulation of feedback is how our games are born.

Looking back, the controller for the Wii, which you can operate one-handed, seems like it was a foregone conclusion, but it was less the result of one person coming up with a great idea and more the uncanny fusion of the scattered thoughts of a large number of people following an unlikely path to its conclusion.

Leading up to the release of the Wii, we produced boxes upon boxes of mock-ups and prototype devices and software, none of which were a waste of time. There was an outpouring of ideas, and when we came upon a handful of fortuitous technologies, all kinds of problems were solved at once.

No one knew at the beginning how the Wii was going to turn out, just that we wouldn't find the answers by sticking to the usual routes. All we knew was the direction we were heading in.

Meanwhile, our time was obviously limited, and it's not like we could slack off on delivering products. If I look back on the way we've gone about things, developing new systems while we put out new handheld consoles, I can cite all kinds of little things throughout the process that I wish we had done differently, but when it comes to the Wii, I'm baffled at the lack of things I feel that way about. I can proudly say, "If I could turn back time, I'd make it the same."

How the two of us made
Super Smash Bros.

The original *Super Smash Bros.* was released in 1999 for the Nintendo 64, but the prototype was created by myself and Masahiro Sakurai.

At that stage, the game didn't include Nintendo characters. Sakurai took care of everything, from the planning and the specs to the design, modeling, and animations, while I did all the programming single-handedly. One other person did the sound. This was basically the ultimate indie game.

HAL Laboratory, where we were working at the time, handled a variety of software, but we were trying to determine our creative focus, the sort of games that only we could make. This was when Sakurai told me that he had a fun idea. I was encouraging and told him, "Put together something quick, so you can play with it. I'll do the programming if you plan everything out."

Both of us had our hands full with other work, so finding the time wasn't easy. I had no time during the week, which meant spending the weekends programming. Sakurai would send the specs and files, and I'd put something together, asking, "Hey, how about this?" We passed the ball back and forth. It was an interesting experience.

After the first round of programming, we knew that we had something special. But at the time, we never dreamed the game would grow to such great heights.

As new titles were added to the *Super Smash Bros.* series, the cast of characters grew and new modes were introduced, so that each installment boasted an exceptional volume of content. In general, I think that making a game bigger is oftentimes not the way to make it better, but with *Super Smash Bros.* I see things differently. It felt right to squeeze as much in there as possible, like some kind of a bottomless vessel, the sort of game where quantity works.

Our motto for *Wario* was "Do whatever Nintendo can't do"

In the early stages of development, we never imagined that the *WarioWare* series would produce such a steady stream of games. This was unexpected in the best possible way, but at the same time, I feel like the *WarioWare* series was a precursor for what is now Nintendo's fundamental stance: approaching new customers.

You could say that *WarioWare* opened the gate to a new path for us. The games have a broad scope, with tons of space to play around, and can be played in short, focused bursts or long, immersive sessions. This broad, dynamic, range of play is incredibly similar to the direction Nintendo is now heading in.

When we were creating *WarioWare*, I remember saying all the time, "We need to do whatever Nintendo hasn't been able to do." Interestingly enough, it was Shigeru Miyamoto who masterminded the release of the first *Wario* title, putting tons of energy into the plan.

Essentially, the idea of "doing what Nintendo can't do" meant "anything Shigeru Miyamoto would probably do," but sure enough, the "impostor" series born from this idea had no stronger backer than Miyamoto himself. What Miyamoto wanted more than anybody was the sort of games that he would never make.

One of these games had a feature I'll never forget. An early version of *WarioWare: Twisted!* included something called the "record player."

The basic premise is you place the Game Boy Advance on a swivel chair, and then you spin the chair around. Sure enough, the record player in the game will spin along with the chair, and as you spin the chair faster and faster, the music in the game speeds up!

I remember sitting there for hours on end, spinning the chair around. Now and then, I'd say, "This is so silly." And yet, I found it so incredibly satisfying. "Silly" is a lofty compliment!

Light users and core users

It was my strong opinion that we needed to call the controller for the Wii a "remote." I was oddly stubborn about this.

My thought was that the television remote, in most houses, is always sitting somewhere close at hand, where anyone can casually pick it up and see what's on. I wanted people to treat a game controller in the same way, which really shows in the final design, to the point where I believed that calling this thing a remote was a done deal.

The question of why everybody in the family will pick up the TV remote but won't pick up a video game controller was a driving concept behind the development of the Wii. That's why I was so insistent that "we absolutely need to call this a remote!"

At this point, nobody has any issues using a cross-shaped control pad or A and B buttons. But in the 1980s, most people would look at a controller and say, "You use this thing to play a game?" The lesson here is that if we do what we need to do, and do it right, the things that today come across as odd will wind up being the new standard.

Most of the games in existence fit into a preexisting framework of video games, but it's worth remembering that we're the ones who gave this framework shape, saying, "If you don't do this, it won't feel like a game."

I felt like it was time we broke free from those old constraints and took a broader approach, however, which is how we came up with "games for strengthening the brain" and "games where you hang out with a dog" and "games for learning English" and "games where you cook food."

I know some people might question whether these are actually games. It's just that the rewards aren't about scores or clearing levels, but changes in your actual life.

That's how Nintendo has been reaching out to people who don't play video games. Of course, we're not ignoring the people who already play games, but unless people who don't play games can see their value, the status of games in society will never improve.

Games have a reputation for being a bad influence, which includes suspect claims like the idea that playing video games too much will mess you up or ruin your brain. As a result, people who like video games can start to feel weirdly guilty for playing them.

If people who don't play video games start playing them and realize how much fun these games can be, there's potential for drastic change. And if the people who play games can feel more comfortable in society, it becomes easier than ever to produce classic games.

While Nintendo has been paying more attention to people who don't usually play games, it's not like we've given up on making games in the classic style, like the latest *Legend of Zelda* game, the result of years of extensive effort. And of course, the passion is as strong as ever.

I think there's value in thinking that you can make something good without spending much in the way of time or resources, which is a principle that came out of the success of the Nintendo DS. At the same time, I also think it's important for people to behold the quality and production level of a game like *Zelda* and realize, "Wow, a ton of experts must have poured their hearts and souls into this!"

Each end of the spectrum benefits from the other's existence. I see this wide range of focus as vital. If we relied on either side, we wouldn't have a healthy balance.

The fact is, I don't think we can think of light users and core users as belonging to completely separate groups. After all, everyone starts off as a light user.

Gaming always begins as a curiosity, but some people will have so much fun they just can't get enough. Yet somehow this idea that light users and core users come from different planets has become all too common. Proponents of this theory overlook all the time involved, and talk as if people are born one way or the other.

But in reality, that's not the case, since even the biggest gaming fans—who demonstrate extraordinary skill—were once light users in their own right.

With that in mind, I think it's so important that new people continue to discover games. Unless we make these games a welcoming space for new audiences, a day will come when people walk away.

IWATA'S WORDS OF WISDOM
PART FIVE

- Sometimes in a game, you'll find a stone just sitting there for no reason. Ask whoever made it "Why did you put this here?" and they're liable to say "Why not?" But "why not" is the worst reason imaginable.

- When you're making a game, at first there are so many things you want to do, but piling on all the features you want won't make the game superior. When you figure out exactly "what is necessary for this game," a world of possibilities will open up. So, rather than tossing in whatever you want, it's good to remember the creative power of paring back.

- Something we're incredibly conscious of with our own platforms is how the hardware and the software combine to establish movement, and the extent to which the same gaming experience can be enjoyed by kids and older folks alike, without them having to read instructions.

- After a piece of hardware is released, the price is gradually reduced for five years until demand has run its course. But since the demand cycle never fails, why bother reducing the price this way? My personal take on the situation is that if you lower the price over time, the manufacturer is conditioning the customer to wait for a better deal, something I've always thought to be a strange approach. Of course, this doesn't mean that I'm against lowering prices entirely, but I've always wanted to avoid a situation where the first people to step up and support us feel punished for paying top dollar, grumbling, "I guess this is the price I pay for being first in line."

- When working on a project, I've found that what really counts is not what you add, but what you throw away and what you decide to leave out. What I find so fascinating is that whenever you're making something, you have this steady stream of chances to incorporate all kinds of technical pieces. But for the most part, you pass them up, deciding "now isn't the time." I'm not sure whether this metaphor is good or bad, but designing hardware is like sitting down at a conveyor belt sushi bar, gazing at all of the different technical pieces making the rounds. Watching them go, you see a piece and say "That one!" and take it off the belt. That's what designing hardware is like for me.

- In the entertainment world, people lose their interest in a unique way that's hard to define.

- Some say that constraint is the mother of creativity.

- A game doesn't need to be like an encyclopedia. As long as you have a good idea and the right angle, it can be closer to a magazine or comic. When putting a game together, it's fundamentally about "if I do this, I can't do that" and "since these two things have that kind of a relationship, they make something interesting when combined." Today's games tend not to revolve around one interesting feature, but complicated combinations. This is what makes them unsatisfying. That's what happens when the design is based on the idea of "more, more, more."

- "The *Zelda* touch" defies explanation, but somehow these incredibly evasive values find a way of making themselves known. At the very least, I can say that what we think of as "*Zelda*" did not just pop out of one person's head, in one piece, but instead is the result of all kinds of people racking their brains and sharing their ideas in various attempts to achieve the *Zelda* touch, which keeps things new and exciting, generating new ideas. In this way, the *Zelda* touch gradually comes into being in the minds of the people who create it. I'm not sure I understand the *Zelda* touch myself, but I think the constant quest, shared by everybody working on these games, to attain the *Zelda* touch speaks to the *Zelda* touch perhaps more than anything.

- In my view, the online games of the world are unfairly biased toward the strong. It takes the bad luck of a hundred or a thousand players to make a single player happy. Of course, I don't mean to dismiss these platforms wholesale, but as long as they retain this element, things will never expand beyond a certain level. As fun as it might look from the outside, most people will drag their heels at the entrance. There has to be another way. I've spent so many years trying to figure out how to make these online games a place where parents can feel comfortable encouraging their kids to play, and how to create a world where harassment is not an issue.

- When people receive feedback about what they've done, they feel more motivated the next time around. But without feedback, nothing is sustainable. Feedback is our reward, what keeps us going. The world of video games uses this to its advantage and is fundamentally designed around the feedback people offer after an experience. This feedback might be pleasant or it might be unpleasant, but the real question is how you can incorporate it to keep these people with you, to keep them interested and excited. This sort of thing is always on my mind when I create.

- A video game is interesting when you can have fun simply watching someone play.

CHAPTER SIX

REMEMBERING IWATA

SHIGERU MIYAMOTO REMEMBERS IWATA: "He wasn't my boss. He was a friend."

orn in 1952, Shigeru Miyamoto is representative director and game creator at Nintendo. He contributed to the development of renowned games such as *Super Mario Bros.* and *The Legend of Zelda* that changed the course of gaming history.

Being good at different things

I think the first time I met Satoru Iwata was in 1988, when we were making *Famicom Grand Prix II: 3D Hot Rally*. At the time, Iwata was director of development at HAL Laboratory, and I knew him as the skilled programmer in charge of previous Nintendo titles like *Golf* and *Balloon Fight*, though we had never actually met in person.

One day, he asked me if I would mind taking a look at this racing game that HAL was making. In keeping with HAL's reputation for technical skill, the game had an audacious course design that you would never see on a real racetrack. The trouble was that it sorely lacked pizzazz. It was a shame to see it go to waste, so I jumped in, made the main character Mario, and reorganized the whole thing as a rally game. Coming together as directors of development for our respective companies and talking through our vision for the game was my first experience of working with Iwata.

He had distinguished himself as a programmer of incredible technical ability, whereas I managed to make up for my, shall we say, lack of technical skill as a developer with my ideas. Of course I envied him for having skills I didn't have, which made working with him so incredibly energizing. I'd like to think Iwata was intrigued by the way that I approached making things, too. It's fun when you're both good at different things. I guess it's reassuring when other people bring strengths you're lacking to the table. I knew for sure that I could trust Iwata. Conversely, if you're both good at the same kind of thing, it's easier to butt heads, and you wind up in all kinds of situations where somebody has to give in. But working with Iwata, I never had to worry about that type of thing.

Take *3D Hot Rally*, for example. Since a 3D racing game would not have been sufficiently exciting on its own, I developed the idea of using characters from the *Mario* franchise and making it a rally game, while Iwata established teams and a course of action for development in consideration of the specialties and strengths of the programmers at his company.

Both of us were producers, but we took charge of different areas. Still, we were trying to make the same thing a reality. And so, if development came to a halt, Iwata could jump-start things with technology, or I could solve things with ideas. Though we relied on different methods, we were after the same thing, and this dynamic continued even after Iwata become president of Nintendo.

The amazing thing about Iwata is that he was so modest about his skill.

His talent and his drive to learn meant he was always getting stronger, but he stayed modest, supporting and encouraging and uplifting other people. When he stepped in to fix a problem, he joined the project as a new member of the team, taking great care not to step on anybody's toes or dishearten anyone involved. This is a really amazing thing to be able to do.

Naming the new

Iwata started up all kinds of great things once he was president of Nintendo, but one thing that stands out was how he gave names to all of the new systems and structures he was making.

When you're developing new hardware, you need to create teams that span departments, but Iwata decided to nickname these groups "roundtables." Having a name like that made the prospect of people coming together from various departments to converse agreeable for everyone involved. They may not have made it onto the organizational chart, but these spaces were defined so that human resources could easily engage with them. Giving things a name helped people to understand their roles intuitively.

This was a major strength of Shigesato Itoi, somebody whom Iwata had long admired, so I think perhaps Iwata took some cues from him. I thought this was a great move, and to this day, I still make a habit of naming even small gatherings or regular meetings. A good name takes on a life of its own, even once the group or organization has dispersed.

When making a decision or starting something up, rather than trying to accomplish everything yourself, it's better to create a group or team with a name that makes the group's objective clear, and work things out together. This is something that Iwata did extremely well.

But it went beyond groups. Naming products is something else that Iwata really poured his heart and soul into. When we released the Wii, he ascribed incredible importance to calling the controller a "remote." Iwata made it thoroughly clear that we needed to adopt the word remote in our official terminology if we were going to appeal to people who had never touched a video game. In a similar vein, it was Iwata's idea to include the word Wii in the titles of games like *Wii Sports* and *Wii Fit*, to make them more approachable to people new to gaming. At the same time, he opted not to do so for the 3DS.

He was the sort of person who gave ample consideration to what would make for a good title, rather than coming up with something on the spot based on feeling.

Iwata had an outstanding ability to summarize and organize ideas. He was precise, and quick too. When naming things, instead of trying to come up with snappy titles, he focused on finding a good way to spell things out and get the point across.

Also, his reading abilities were astounding, allowing him to rapidly evaluate a program. Obviously he was a skilled programmer in his own right, but he truly excelled at reading other people's programs and solving problems. This enabled him to fix or rewrite code with ease. I think this must have been due to his powers of inference, and how he genuinely enjoyed reading a program and figuring out what the programmer was trying to do based on the way it was written. It wasn't so much a drive to learn as an enjoyment of the learning process.

Oh yeah, and he typed on the keyboard insanely fast. I tried to follow his example, but it was no use. I couldn't keep up!

Difference without antagonism

Let's just say I'm not accustomed to receiving compliments ... but Iwata complimented me all the time, like I was some kind of a prince. He made a habit of calling himself my "number one follower," often remembering things verbatim that I had no recollection of saying. I may have been the one who said, "A good idea is something that solves multiple problems in a flash," but Iwata was the one who spread the word.

He seemed to take great interest in the starting point of my ideas and how I began creating a project, and talked about this stuff with people all the time. But rather than ask me directly, he searched for answers on his own. He seemed to enjoy it, too! I used to tell him he was already extremely skilled in so many ways. "Can't you get along without mastering this too?"

That said, his creative capacity was immense, and he laid the entire groundwork for games like the *Brain Age* series. The approach, exemplified by so many DS games of the era, where you started with a theme that then gave shape to an idea, was something that he had come up with on his own.

Whereas I tend to think in terms of how people will physically or emotionally respond, starting a project from ideas like "This sort of thing will probably make people feel this way" or "People will love it if we do this," Iwata's projects were based more on concrete themes. In this case, he realized the power of language like "brain training," that people feel uneasy if you say their brain needs exercise, and that proposing steps to keep their brain from atrophying would be a source of motivation, which he took as his starting point for planning. He didn't brood over hazy ideas, but was constantly searching for themes with catalytic potential. Same goes for when he was developing new hardware.

Iwata and I may think about and make things differently, but this never once resulted in a full-blown argument. Even when we had a difference of opinion, we were able to bounce ideas off of each other, testing each other's outlook and experience in the best way possible.

Probably the one thing that we clearly disagreed on was our interpretation of the dress code! Iwata cared a great deal about this sort of thing, and even when there wasn't any rule in place he came up with one and stuck to his own standards so as not to offend others. In contrast, my personal opinion is that nobody really cares. Since Iwata was the highest-ranking person at the company, I guess he sometimes had to take a stern approach, but his approach to laxness and strictness was unique.

Working together on *Pokémon Snap*

It was rare for Iwata and me to commit ourselves to the same game, but a notable exception was with *Pokémon Snap* for Nintendo 64, where we were both deeply involved.

That game got its start as the "Jack and the Beanstalk Project," a game that Nintendo was helping its outside contractors to create, where you take photos with a camera, but at a certain stage of development we hit an impasse, at a loss as to how to bring it all together.

I was working to make the photo-taking aspect more robust, but Iwata stressed that while a game where you take photos was a decent start, what really mattered was what you could photograph." Then, at one point, he told me, "Miyamoto, I think it's Pokémon. That's what the people really want to photograph." I thought this was a great idea, and this became the guiding principle for the game. In summary, Iwata contributed the idea that what everybody wanted to photograph was Pokémon, while it was my job to construct an interesting system for taking all these photographs, making this one of our closest collaborations.

Normally, our conversations focused not so much on explicitly collaborative tasks, but on the fostering of big picture ideas. When one of us would show up with a project in the works, we tended to see eye to see about how it was working out. For example, it's all well and good for something to come together really smoothly, a really tidy product with no noticeable errors, but Iwata and I both questioned the merits of going to the trouble of creating something so innocuous as that. When that happens, it's a huge boon to have someone beside you who agrees.

Iwata and I may have generally seen eye to eye when it came to major judgment calls about the games, but our standards for evaluating things differed remarkably. He was constantly pointing out these details I had completely

overlooked about the greater context of a project, which
kept things interesting.

When passing judgment on things, the knowledge you
possess will form your standard of evaluation, but being able
to augment that with another, different set of standards
you can count on is a really valuable thing.

Books, meetings, and a spirit of service

One major change in Iwata, after leaving HAL Laboratory to
become president of Nintendo, is that he started reading books
on business. Despite having no time, he read tons of books,
and if he found a good one, he would recommend we all read
it too. I'm not really a book-reading kind of guy, but I made
a habit of reading the books Iwata strongly recommended.

Iwata didn't read in search of hints on how to do things,
but to find support for the ideas that constituted his
worldview, and so that he could use books as a resource for
conveying these ideas to others. He was always pondering
the meaning of what Nintendo was doing, and the circumstances in which the company found itself at any given
time, so when he found something that validated what he
was thinking in a book that he was reading, it strengthened
his resolve. By recommending that employees read these
books, he was able to explain his ideas and unify the vision of
the company. This is how he put these books to use. Sometimes

this meant buying a few books for those around him, and other times it meant giving a recommended reading list to everybody at the company.

Among the books he recommended, one that made a deep impression on me was a book about behavioral economics. Until Iwata pointed me in this direction, I had no idea the field even existed, but I immediately recognized what I was reading. "Wow, so this is what you call what we've been doing all along!" I guess Iwata was bowled over by the revelation as well, and immediately read a ton more books in order to enrich his understanding. When I saw him, he'd say things like "This is exactly what Nintendo has been doing" or "This is along the same lines of your philosophy, Miyamoto," explaining it to me in simple terms. At times I wondered why he didn't write a book like this himself!

Apart from books, another thing Iwata really valued as a president was bringing people together for meetings. In no time, he managed to impress upon the company the importance of his role as a facilitator.

In his view, a facilitator was a person who ensured that meetings were productive, adding a touch of creativity where it was lacking, or focusing the conversation when there was an excess of creativity. Effectively, it meant being the producer of a meeting. He made an effort to impress upon the company the importance, in any kind of meeting, of having a facilitator who was there to help the meeting show results. This sometimes meant tapping a specific person and saying, "I need you to be the facilitator for this team." It's interesting how being called upon to serve as a facilitator can expand your knowledge base.

Iwata left all kinds of legacies like this behind him, ideas that became woven into the very fabric of the company. One thing's for sure, though—Iwata loved seeing the company work better thanks to something that he introduced. I think he saw this less as the job of a president, and more like an act of service. Nothing pleased him more than hearing, "Thanks to you, things are going well."

"Visual control" and company-wide interviews

Iwata also made an effort to proactively convey to the employees the sort of decisions that he and the company directors were making based on these new ways of thinking. He used the term "visual control" all the time, and made an effort to employ it in his management of Nintendo.

This applied not only to things like distributing minutes and holding essential meetings, but also to planning events that catered to the interests of the employees, inviting like-minded individuals from outside the company to speak before the staff, and making adjustments so that people could share all kinds of information in an enjoyable manner.

For example, at one board of directors meeting, we re-moved the desks and chairs from one corner of the room and set up a big television. Then we had the factory manager, who didn't actually play games much, try out our newest sports game. Before long, he was having a great time, drenched in sweat and saying, "Whoa, we gotta make a ton of these!" This is just one example of how we turned our attention toward setting up frameworks for sharing information in interesting ways.

In this respect, one thing Iwata really valued was meeting one-on-one.

Since he had been doing these meetings since his time at HAL Laboratory, I know it must have been a high priority for him, and after becoming president, he made a point of sitting down with every employee working on development. There must have been over two hundred people.

These systematic interviews were not some bureaucratic requirement. They were part of Iwata's personal management style. As applies to so many other things we've discussed, Iwata did this out of genuine curiosity. As a result, everyone cooperated, and no one felt like they were being forced to participate. I think Iwata's hope was that each person would be encouraged to think for themselves.

Wondering if Iwata ever got angry? Actually, no. At least, he never raised his voice or anything like that. Sure, he could be strict at times. But if some kind of problem threw a monkey wrench into production and our customers were waiting, he was less upset about the problem than the feeling that he couldn't offer customers a proper explanation.

Something that Iwata and I had in common is impatience with people saying that they're "doing all they can" when no kind of a solution has been reached. You might be doing everything you're supposed to do, in terms of company and interpersonal responsibilities, but if nothing has been solved for those depending on you, all you've done is provoke their anxiety. It upset Iwata when we kept a customer waiting by saying something like, "We'll need to circle back with our supply chain before we can provide an answer," and let me tell you, it upset me too!

The Iwata I knew

When Iwata and I sat down together and talked, regardless of how strongly we disagreed, he never got the least bit irritated. Sometimes he was at a loss for words, though. He'd talk forever, really on a roll, then suddenly go quiet. I think these were the moments where we disagreed.

But Iwata wasn't formulating a counterargument—he was thinking. Seeing where his thoughts would take him. In that sense, a disagreement would become a point of focus. After a while, he'd finally say, "About that..." And I'd say, "Oh, you were thinking the whole time!"

That's part of what made Iwata such an interesting person.

He had a hunger to process raw materials, or any kind of input. This applied to books as well, but also to the substance of our lunchtime conversations. He took great interest in all of the different obstacles and discoveries of development.

A week later, we'd be having lunch again and he would say, "I think I've figured out your problem."

That's something about Iwata's personality that never changed from the time that we first met. It never changed a bit.

One of the first times we worked together, when Iwata was visiting Kyoto from HAL Laboratory in Yamanashi, we lost track of time and worked late into the night, so we stepped out for some ramen. Nintendo doesn't go in for wining and dining as a policy, so after eating out like this a few times we began to split the bill as a general rule, and kept that going even once he was the president and I was a director. Splitting the bill, for twenty years! Iwata never changed the way he cultivated his relationships and lived his life. I remember us eating ramen like a couple of maniacs in the middle of the night. That was a lot of fun. Though I guess the total of the dinner bills may have increased a bit over the years!

When it all comes down to it, Iwata was my friend. He never bossed me around, got mad at me, or fought with me. At any other company, you might expect there to be some tension when a younger person with less experience passes you and becomes president, but in our case there was nothing of the sort. Once he came over and we started to work together in the same company, I realized, "This guy's way more fit to be the president." I'm glad that things turned out that way.

Like I said, we really became friends. In no time flat.

What else is there to say, I wonder? At home, he was respected as a father. I envied him for having a family like that. His wife is such a gentle soul. Because there wasn't much chance during the day for exercise, he put a treadmill in the president's office so he could jog. He also played *Wii Fit* all the time. I have all these different memories, and they come back to me at random moments.

One major way in which we differed is that whenever he was on the Shinkansen or on an airplane, he loved to make effective use of his free time. Meanwhile, I'd be slacking off, asleep before we were underway. When we visited Europe, he would tell me that if I could sleep through the whole red-eye flight out of Haneda we could start work first thing in the morning, in Paris, as if this was the best thing in the world.

By the way, did you know that we sometimes called Iwata "Kirby" at the office? If you're stuck in a long meeting, and there's a pile of candy, it's easy to eat a ton, right? Well, doing that earned him the nickname "Kirby," and we made sure there was always lots of candy close at hand.

And another thing: Iwata hated Japanese pickles. To be honest, I'm the same way. The only difference is that in my case, most people don't know. When Shigesato Itoi came to Kyoto, we tended to go out to dinner at the same spot, and this place made milder pickles that both Iwata and I agreed were the only delicious pickles in existence. We never said so at the time, but a number of years after we had started going there, he said to me, "Those are the only ones I like," and I said, "Same here!"

Iwata may have passed on, but the company is going strong. Thanks to all the ideas and systems that he left behind, our young hires have been able to thrive. What makes me sad is that if I have a crazy idea over the weekend, there isn't anybody I can tell about it on Monday morning.

When I'm eating lunch, he isn't there to say, "I think I've figured out your problem," which leaves me feeling stuck sometimes. I really miss him.

SHIGESATO ITOI REMEMBERS IWATA: "He wanted to make everybody happy."

Born in 1948, Shigesato Itoi is the copywriter and editor in chief of *Hobo Nikkan Itoi Shinbun*. His wide variety of creative projects range from designing games to writing lyrics. He became acquainted with Satoru Iwata through their work on *EarthBound*. It was the start of a close friendship.

My trust deepened
every time we met

The first time I met Iwata was when we were developing
EarthBound. Before that, we had never even said hello or
exchanged a few passing words. Hiroshi Yamauchi, the
former president of Nintendo, had asked me several times
"Have you met Iwata yet?" and insisted that "You two
should meet," but the opportunity never seemed to arise.
Funny thing is, when I asked Iwata about this years later,
sure enough Yamauchi had been saying the exact same thing
to him: "You two should meet!"

So, when *EarthBound* started having problems and we
were having difficulty pushing forward with development,
we asked Iwata for help. We met in Tokyo at the offices of
Ape Inc., which was initially responsible for developing the
game. I explained exactly what condition *EarthBound* was
in and told Iwata everything, including what sort of role he
might play in the process.

Once I was finished, Iwata told me something that has
gone down in history:

"Working with what we have, it would take two years to
fix things up. If you don't mind starting from scratch, we
could be done in half a year."

Of course, we let him start from scratch. A little over a
year later, after adding the finishing touches, *EarthBound*
was released into the world, an unimaginable feat for

anybody with intimate knowledge of how messy things had been. I couldn't have been happier.

It's hard to find the words, but my first impression of Iwata was extremely pleasant. We had no history, but I was so on board with everything he said. Years later, Iwata confessed that he was "pretty nervous at the time," but he didn't come across that way at all. "Should we fix it the way it is? Or should we start from scratch?" When I see those words in print they almost come across as insolent, but there was nothing remotely pushy about them. He made me feel as if he took great stock in my freedom to make the decision. We had asked him for help getting things going, but I found his attitude even more inspiring than his technical approach, and as we continued to meet, I came to trust him more and more.

Not to focus too much on myself, but once Iwata started coming by I had to keep my wits about me, since he made me feel responsible in the best way possible. At the time my main work was as a copywriter, and despite having spent years working on video games, I still saw them as something that I did for fun. This can have a positive effect on the creative side of things, but on the whole it leaves the project vulnerable to collapse. Then Iwata showed up, showing no traces of arrogance or frustration, grinning as he got us on our feet. All the same, I could tell that he was definitely not taking it easy, which naturally compelled me to take on more responsibility.

On a broader level, I think we were only able to turn things around like that because Iwata had replenished our sense of hope by saying, "We can do this."

Iwata never changed, from that first impression right through his time as president of Nintendo. Though I guess Miyamoto said the same thing earlier!

Ensuring an environment for all

One thing that stuck with me about the way Iwata salvaged *EarthBound* is how he started off by creating the tools he needed to fix the game.

After announcing it would be done in half a year, he didn't simply shut the door and fix the game himself. Rather, he set up systems so that the entire staff could fix the game together. I was astonished by the freshness of this approach.

It was like he'd parachuted in and rescued us, so he could have easily shown off his abilities and insisted that we let him take care of everything, but rather than single-handedly pulling us out of the crisis, in a way that would depend on his authority, he created an environment where everyone had access to the content of the game. This made each of us certain that "we can do this if we try." Once everybody felt like things would work out if we put the effort in, the sense of relief was incredible.

Iwata also coined the phrase "Programmers should never say no," which later became infamous. Iwata was worried that the message had taken on a life of its own and caused a lot of people grief, but obviously this was not what he had intended when he said it. Rather, he was saying something like "It's our job to think up ways of giving ideas shape so that Itoi can feel free to share his vision openly." That meant so much to me.

Iwata was also good at responding to ideas. When I tossed out a wild idea, being my usual smart aleck self, he'd look entertained and say something like "I never would have thought of that" or "Should we have a go at it?" Sometimes he'd even say, "If we did that, we could do this," responding with another new idea. This led to the graphical presentation in the Lost Underworld and the invention of "eraser" items for eliminating obstacles.

Another thing that I remember Iwata saying is "Anything a computer can do for you should be left to a computer." Maybe this is obvious to people who can leverage computers on a daily basis, but to me it was a revelation. Iwata often said, "People only want to do things only people can do," and I think that he was exactly right. Iwata was probably better at using computers than anyone, but he never used his expertise to set himself above others. Instead, I got the sense that he was interested mostly in the things that only human beings can do because of all the work computers could take off their hands.

When I look back on the nitty-gritty of development for *EarthBound*, I don't remember speaking with Iwata in great detail about the content of the game. Since things like the script and the dialogue had been created separately, he was able to draw from this material as he pleased. The times when I chimed in and said, "I'd like for us to try this,"

Iwata said, "Okay, let's do it this way," immediately supporting the idea. I don't really have any memory of either of us insisting that it "should be this way" or discussing "what a video game is supposed to do." Admittedly, that could just mean that I've forgotten! What I do remember is discussing fundamentals, like what people would find interesting.

When it got late, and Iwata had to make the trip home to Yamanashi, I often saw him off at the south exit of Shinjuku Station. Most nights, he took the Azusa limited express train, talking to himself about the "bumpy ride" as he rubbed elbows with the folks carrying hiking gear, while genuinely enjoying the ride home.

Like a younger brother, no matter the setting

Iwata was about ten years younger than me, but I think he probably felt a little on the young side, regardless of the situation. I mean, he had become president of HAL Laboratory in his early thirties, and the president of Nintendo by age forty-two.

He was certainly a leader, but he was also like family. Even after becoming the president of a huge company like Nintendo, he still acted like a younger brother in noticeable ways. Not in the sense of being immature, but in his tendency to put everybody else's needs before his own. When he had something to propose, it never came out like an order or some kind of decree, but like he was putting in his two cents, like he was saying, "After thinking things over, I'm wondering if we could try it this way."

It felt like the age difference between Iwata and me allowed for both of us to relax. Though I can't speak to what his feelings were.

I'm remembering a time when Iwata really came across like a younger brother. We were planning a party, just after the release of *EarthBound.* As we were going back and forth, Iwata said, "If you don't mind, I have a special request," which was unusual for him. I had to chuckle when he wound up asking, "Would you mind bringing your wife [actress Kanako Higuchi] to the party?" My wife doesn't usually show up for these kinds of things, but when I explained the situation, she obliged and came along. As it turned out, Iwata was something of a fanboy!

There was another time, which must have been around the release of *EarthBound,* when Iwata asked me to share my thoughts with the employees of HAL Laboratory, so I drove out to Yamanashi on the Chuo Expressway and gave a kind of lecture to the company. I usually refuse all speaking offers as a rule, but when Iwata asked, I couldn't refuse.

We kept in touch long after *EarthBound,* until one day he asked if I would serve as a consultant for HAL Laboratory. Iwata visited my company and divulged every facet of his approach to work, saying that he wanted me to understand where he was coming from before making a decision. When

Iwata asked me I was already ready to say yes, but I heard him out, just like he wanted.

Most of what he had to say involved happiness.

I realized he'd been saying this kind of thing the whole time. He was the sort of person who wanted to make everybody happy. He wanted to be happy, like he wanted his friends to be happy and his customers to be happy. I think I told him that I liked how he used the English word "happy," though he pronounced it like a Japanese word whenever he said it. I shared his sentiment completely and was so thrilled to hear him say these things.

This part of the memory is so goofy that I hesitate to mention it, but every time Iwata said the word "happy," he spread his fingers wide, like he was smiling with both hands. I'll never forget that about him.

That day was fun. Just the two of us, talking for hours.

Always talking, because he was having fun

After Iwata become president of Nintendo I started making regular visits to Kyoto, so we had many more chances to meet up. I think I saw him almost every time I visited, and Iwata frequently stopped by the office for a chat when he was on a trip to Tokyo. Even when time was short, we both found room in our schedules.

Whenever we met up, we talked for the entire time. To the point where my wife told me once, "Men sure are chatterboxes!"

When we met up in Kyoto, we might head into town on some kind of an errand, then chat for a while over food, after which we'd head over to his house and chat some more. Iwata would start tossing his dog a ball while we were talking. Then his wife would take the dog out for a walk, only to come home and find us still talking. In our longest session, I arrived at lunch and talked with him until maybe nine at night. Iwata's wife must have been wondering what was up with these two goofballs.

If you're wondering what we spent so much time discussing in Kyoto, or in Tokyo, it was mainly whatever had been on our minds. Someone would start off with "I've been thinking," and from there the other guy would say "I've thought about that too!" or maybe "In that case, I think you could do this," so in a sense these chats were similar to meetings. None of this involved actual work, of course, but we were really grappling with these questions! It never took the form of heated debate. It was more like we applied gentle pressure to each other's ideas. Not so much "In that case, what about this," but more like "What if you take that even further?" It was a lot of fun. Though perhaps a bit unusual!

When we were riding on the Shinkansen together, we'd be talking the whole time, except I'd nod off now and then. Iwata never slept on trains, so he just kept on talking. When that happened, I'd tell him honestly, "Sorry, man, I'm going to sleep." At that point, Iwata would pull out his laptop and start clicking away. This happened more times than I can count.

One of the great things about him was that he never held back. He also never put on airs, or acted angry just for show. Nothing like that. That's why the two of us could talk for hours, just us guys, without it going sour. I see this as a reflection of Iwata's goodness.

He really was a decent guy, you know? Anybody, man or woman, who you can spend a lot of time alone with is probably a decent person.

I've said as much to Iwata myself, and I mean this in the best sense of the word, but he was a bit of a goofball. But believe me, this was a strength for him. I tend to think that anyone who's met Iwata would agree with me. And if someone told me, "It's not like you're all that sophisticated," I'd probably agree with them. I think this was one of the things we had in common, proof of how the sides we showed each other were compatible.

The friends I spend most of my time with may have changed over the years, but if you add up all the hours, I'd say I've spent the most time with Iwata.

Even sick, Iwata was himself

We had a chance to talk a lot about him getting sick.

When he was diagnosed, I happened to be staying in Kyoto for a short while. That day, I had plans to go out to eat with someone else. Iwata asked me, "Is it okay if I tag along?" This was out of character for him. Since he was usually reserved, he almost never asked that kind of thing. My plans were with a friend who was basically family, so I urged him to join us.

But once we were together, Iwata didn't say a word about his diagnosis. It must have been hard to broach the subject when we were having a good time. Later on, after my daughter got engaged, we were in Kyoto for a dinner, and he asked me once again, "Can we meet up?" That's when he finally told me he was sick. He couldn't call or text me about it. Some things need to be said face-to-face. Afterward, he changed the subject to what sort of wedding present he should give my daughter.

As time went by, we talked a lot about what he was going through, but true to character, Iwata was set on doing his utmost to get better while planning for the possibility of another outcome. He told me, "They have this therapy that I could try." As you can imagine, Iwata had done his homework! We stayed in touch via text, and I'd go to sit beside him at the hospital. Or, if they let him go home for a few days, I would meet him at his house. I want to make sure I respect his privacy, but I can tell you he was always like himself. Except he wasn't wearing his suit...

When he passed away, his wife reached out to let me know, and I had a chance to say goodbye to him, laid out to rest, before the service, dressed up again in one of the suits he always wore. Looking back, I can't believe how young he was. It's such a shame. Of course, I was a little younger then myself, but Iwata was way younger, so much younger than I am today.

All the same, I know that I was on the outside looking in. The weight of my emotions was incomparable to what those who worked alongside him must have felt, and above all what his wife and family went through.

The day of Iwata's funeral service is one I'll never forget. It was a torrential downpour. Shigeru Miyamoto and I were waiting together, and I looked at him and asked him: "What do you think Iwata thought his odds were of getting better?"

Without a second thought, Miyamoto said to me, in the most natural way, "I think he thought he'd make a full recovery, and had no plans of dying whatsoever." Since this was the impression of a person very near to him, I felt our distance all too keenly. Those close to him could see this as a given. I knew for certain that Miyamoto was fully in touch with how Iwata felt about these things.

This is difficult to express, but I think distance has a way of letting facts obscure a situation. Those close at hand, however, have access to a much rawer set of emotions. The instant I heard Miyamoto say those words, I felt ashamed for asking. Though I knew my shame wasn't doing anybody any good.

You know, I feel like our connection is forever.

It's strange how the time when Iwata was alive, the time when he was sick, the time when I received the call about the funeral, and the time when Miyamoto and I spoke are all connected. Those long afternoons in Kyoto, chatting with Iwata until dark, will never leave me.

Fostering happiness

Having known Iwata for years, I had a chance to meet his family many times, and you could tell immediately that he was a good father. After he passed, I'll never forget the way his son came out and said, "He was a good dad to us at home." It's not often a father is recognized like that by his son in Japan.

A fun fact about the two of them is that Iwata and his son both had a habit of walking around when they were thinking about things. And if they were both thinking at the same time, walking around the same room, sometimes they bumped into each other! When his wife told me that story on one of my visits with his family, Iwata laughed and shook his head and said, "She's right!"

His son is now married, but when he and his girlfriend were first dating, I guess his mother saw them walking around town from her car. By her account, their son "was smiling in a way he didn't smile at home," and when Iwata told me this story, he was smiling from ear to ear. I remember his expression even better than the story. He went so far as saying, "His old man's never even seen him smile like that!" I don't think I'd ever heard Iwata call himself "old man" before. That should tell you how amused he was.

Iwata thoroughly enjoyed seeing people smile. This was behind his management philosophy for Nintendo. I think his life's work was to foster happiness.

And he was the kind of guy who spared no effort to achieve that goal. He loved supporting people, loved to understand things, and loved the communication so essential to the process.

That's what made his Monday lunches with Miyamoto so important to him. They were a combination of all the things he loved. A chance for him to say "I think I've got it" and work through an idea that would make his close acquaintances and customers smile.

When he came by our office in Tokyo, he always had a slew of ideas, hypotheses, and thoughts, which he was thrilled to share with me. As the head of the company, he probably should have had somebody with him, but he always showed up in a taxi, by himself, pulling a roller bag, and said "Hello!" in that high voice of his.

CHAPTER SEVEN

IWATA, THE PERSON

Unable to let questions go unasked

've always enjoyed seeking out a reason why. As a kid, I read the encyclopedia from cover to cover. In the process, I'd discover connections between things I didn't understand. I found that so rewarding. It's a lot of fun when all these things you don't know come together and start making sense. I still feel that today!

When I have a question about something, I try to come up with a hypothesis for what's happening. From there, I test out every pattern I can possibly conceive of, and I won't give up until I'm sure that "this explains it all, no matter how you look at it." When I'm sure "this is the answer."

That's why I can't help but investigate when I come across a why that has no explanation. If something inexplicable shows up in what I thought to be the answer, it means that my hypothesis was mistaken—in which case, there has to be some factor that I've overlooked. I'll have to think up a new hypothesis. And so, I start to think again.

If I come up with an answer to a question right away, it probably means I've thought about that thing before.

When it's something that I've thought about before that I feel ready to address, the next step is to try out what I have in mind, but if unresolved concerns start popping up, I have to test out any new hypothesis, even the ones that have just occurred to me.

Since I've worked with computers for so many years, I'm fond of the way logic bars contradiction. When I'm faced with a new question, my first thought is, "How does my answer square with everything I've done up to now?"

Even when I firmly believe "this is the right way to go," I'll need to think things over from all kinds of different angles, or else I'm unwilling to say so.

This way of thinking has the bonus effect of substantively increasing my abilities.

I'm unable to let questions go unasked. Once I'm curious, I want to know the answers. As a result, if someone else can do something and I can't, I start thinking of how I might become able to do it, and taking the steps to get myself there.

That being said, this isn't the sort of thing where I grit my teeth and try as hard as possible. Taking little steps, I'll try out different things, and if I find myself saying, "Hey, I think I'm getting the idea, this is fun," I take this tiny victory as a sign of personal development, and that reward allows me to go even further. Each step is so incredibly small, but as things start making sense and coming together, the effort that you're putting in becomes enjoyable, and with repetition you begin to pick things up.

IWATA'S WORDS OF WISDOM
PART SIX

- On my business card, I am a corporate president. In my mind, I am a game developer. But in my heart, I am a gamer.

- I always want to find a way to be involved. In every case, I'd rather be involved than be a bystander. Whether that means helping somebody in need, or making someone smile, or making customers happy, I want to be involved, contributing to the solution. I cringe at the thought of acknowledging a chance to be involved but staying out of it, telling myself, "I know if I chipped in, things would get better, that I could make a positive contribution, but I don't think it's worth the effort." That's not the way I've lived my life. Refusing to turn down these chances has been difficult at times, but it's also led me to all kinds of interesting things. My thought is that I want to live with no regrets, and use all of the energy I have.

- Since way back when, my motto has been "Whenever I work with someone, I want them to say, 'I'd love to work with you again next time.'" I'm deeply invested in making this come true. The last thing I'd want is for them to say they'd just as soon never see me again.

- In reality, nothing can be created without some degree of hardship. But I think the fact that our staff doesn't come across as overserious is part of what allows us to make products that people can enjoy with smiles on their faces.

- It makes me happy when people have fun playing our video games, but I'm not hoping for other amusements to fall by the wayside. I want people to play video games, but I also want them to experience other kinds of games from an early age. When I was little, I had fun playing all kinds of different ways, and I truly value those experiences.

- When releasing something new, it's thrilling to imagine how the world is going to receive it. It's always like this, whenever we release things. It's scary, every time. That's why I think it's always worth a try.

- No part of my experience has turned out to be a waste of time.

SOURCES OF THE TEXT

The words of Satoru Iwata found in this book have been extracted from various sources published on the *Hobo Nikkan Itoi Shinbun* website, and from the "Iwata Asks" series featured on the Nintendo website. The original content can be viewed (in Japanese) via the following links:

Hobo Nikkan Itoi Shinbun

"Index of content related to Satoru Iwata"
https://www.1101.com/iwata20150711/index.html

Nintendo

"Index of 'Iwata Asks' Links"
https://www.nintendo.co.jp/corporate/links/index.html

SATORU IWATA

Satoru Iwata was born in Hokkaido on December 6, 1959. He graduated from the Tokyo Institute of Technology School of Engineering with a degree in computer science and entered HAL Laboratory upon graduation. In 1993, he became president of HAL Laboratory. In 2000, he joined Nintendo as the head of its corporate planning division. In 2002, he became the president of Nintendo. Iwata brought a number of legendary games into the world during his time as a developer. Then, as the president of Nintendo, he oversaw the creation of legendary game systems like the Nintendo DS and the Wii, venturing all the while, in his own words, "to expand the gaming population."

Selected Works

Pinball

Golf

F1 Race

Balloon Fight

Famicom Grand Prix II: 3D Hot Rally

Kirby's Adventure

EarthBound

Super Smash Bros.

Pokémon Snap

Super Smash Bros. Melee

Brain Age

SAM BETT

Sam Bett is a writer and Japanese translator. Awarded Grand Prize in the 2016 JLPP International Translation Competition, he won the 2019/2020 Japan-U.S. Friendship Commission Prize for his translation of *Star* by Yukio Mishima (New Directions, 2019). Sam has translated fiction by Yoko Ogawa, NISIOISIN, and Keigo Higashino, as well as essays by Fuminori Nakamura, Haruomi Hosono, and Banana Yoshimoto. He is also a founder and host of Us&Them, a quarterly Brooklyn-based reading series show-casing the work of writers who translate. With David Boyd, he is cotranslating the novels of Mieko Kawakami for Europa Editions. He lives in Portland, Maine.

❝ No part of my experience has turned out to be a waste of time.❞

SATORU IWATA